Horses in Art

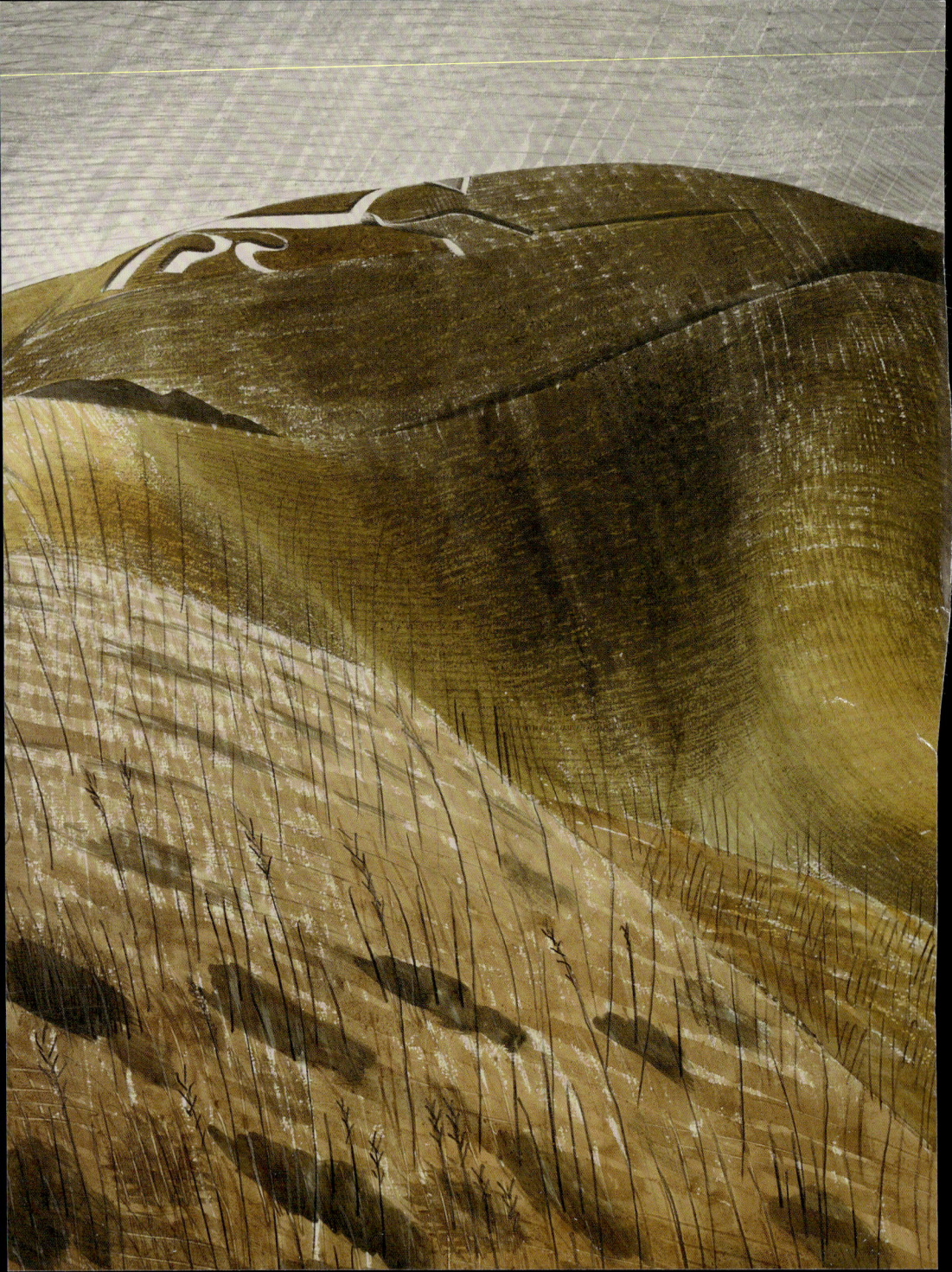

CHIEDZA MHONDORO

Horses
in Art

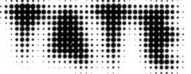

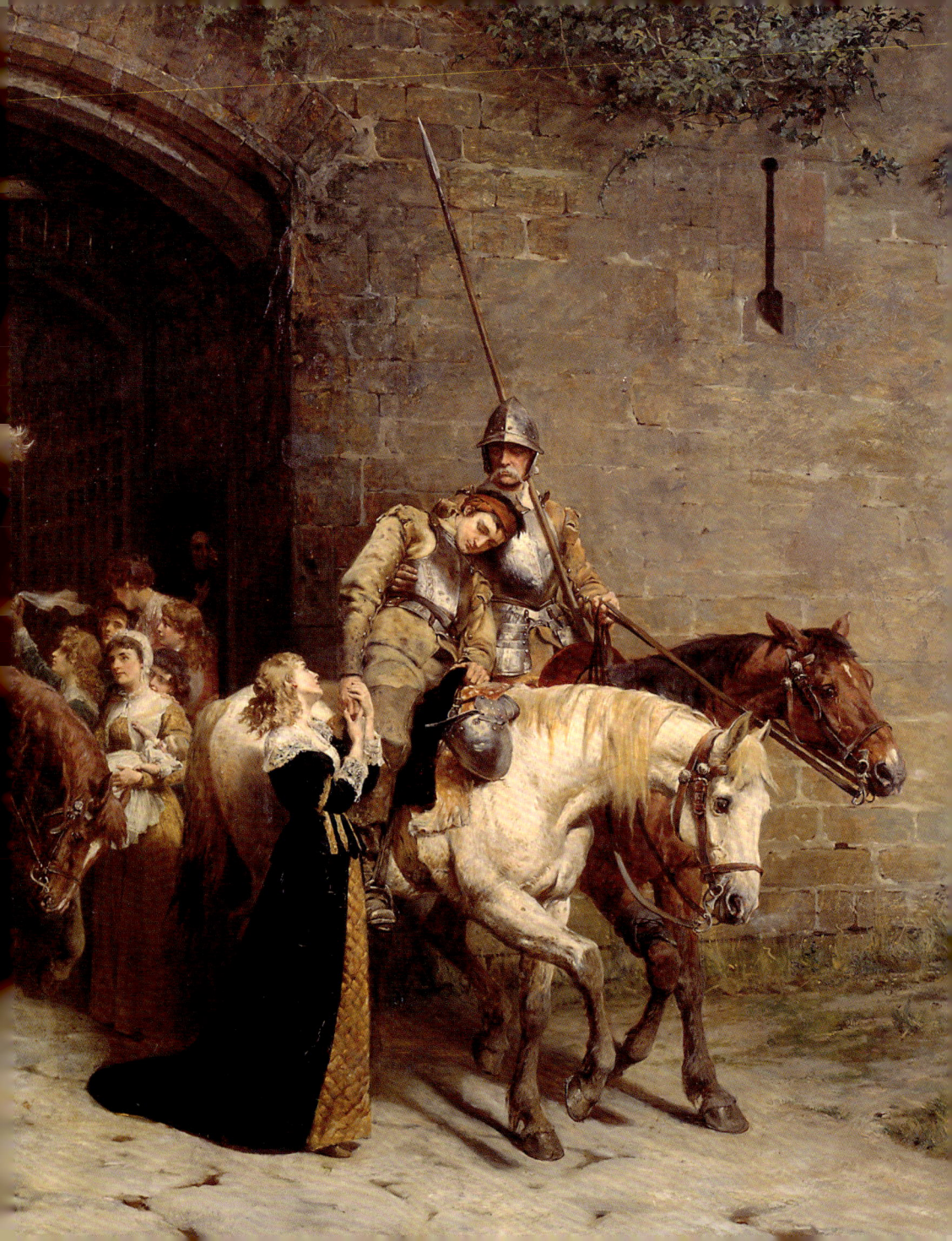

A Brief History of Horses in Art

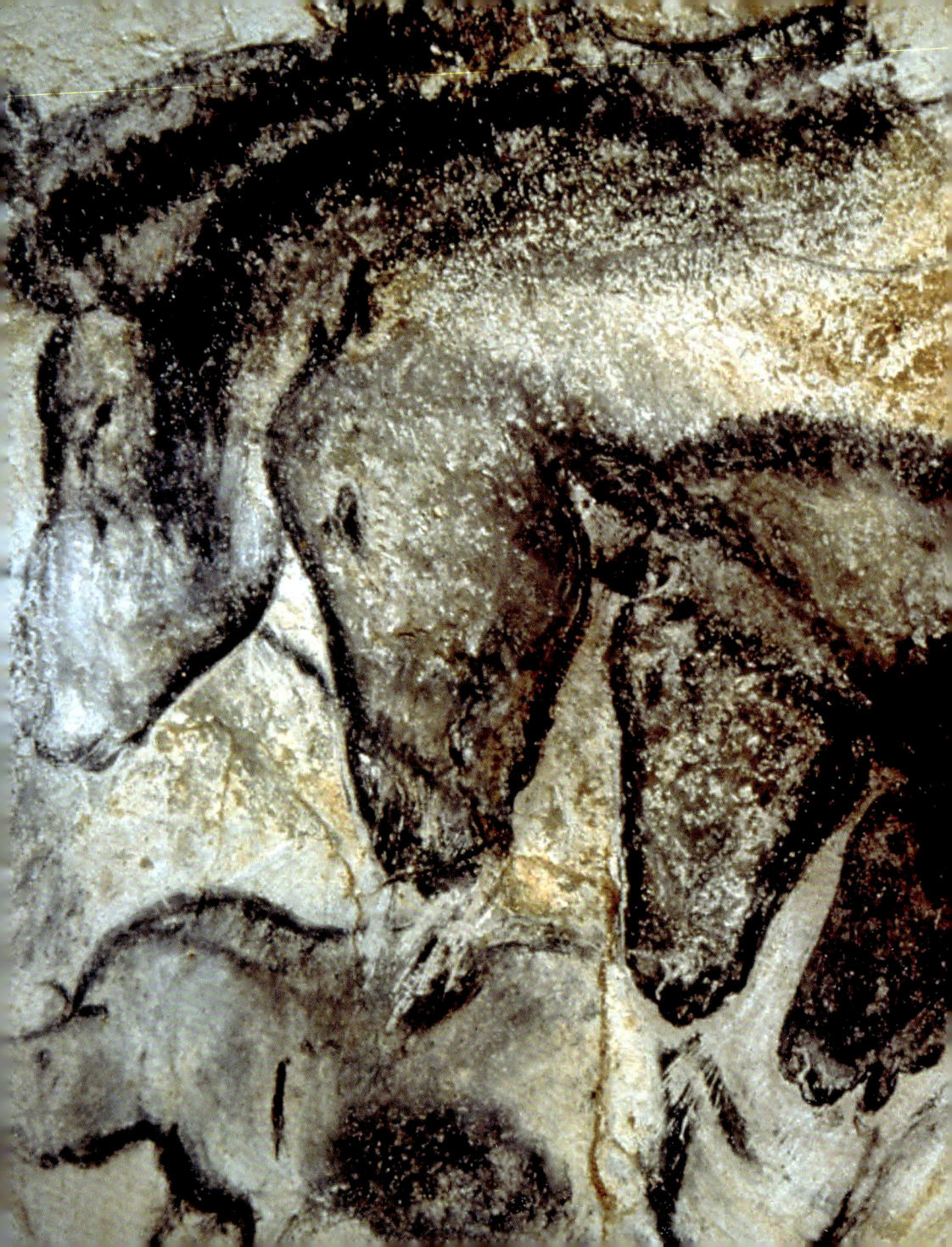

A Brief History of
Horses in Art

Around 32,000 years ago in Ardèche, south-eastern France, our ancestors painted four wild horses on the walls of the vast Chauvet Cave, the home of one of the earliest known examples of prehistoric art (left). The charcoal portraits show the horses in profile with thick necks and short, stiff, upright manes. All four are stocky and the one closest to us is open-mouthed and alert. They appear three-dimensional as a result of the artist's shading. The execution of the cave painting is clear and sophisticated, rendering the animals instantly recognisable. To date, over twenty horses have been found within the Chauvet Cave, along with images of rhinos, lions, mammoths, bison, reindeer and oxen.

Deep in the Lascaux Cave on the other side of France, around 15,000 BCE, another wave of Palaeolithic artists painted horses on the walls and ceilings. Their horses are also uniquely depicted, in a palette of black, warm browns, yellows and reds. The caves that house these paintings are difficult to access from the main entrance; many of the chambers are hard to enter, and are likely to have been visited for religious or ceremonial purposes. With no written records, it remains a mystery why early humans were compelled to glorify horses on their stone canvases with such boldness, clarity and care.

Detail of the *Panel of the Horses* in the Chauvet-Pont d'Arc cave, France, c.32,000 BCE. Overleaf, relief fragment: *cavalrymen along a stream in mountainous terrain*, c.704-681 BCE, gypsum alabaster, 54.5 × 87.8 × 12.8

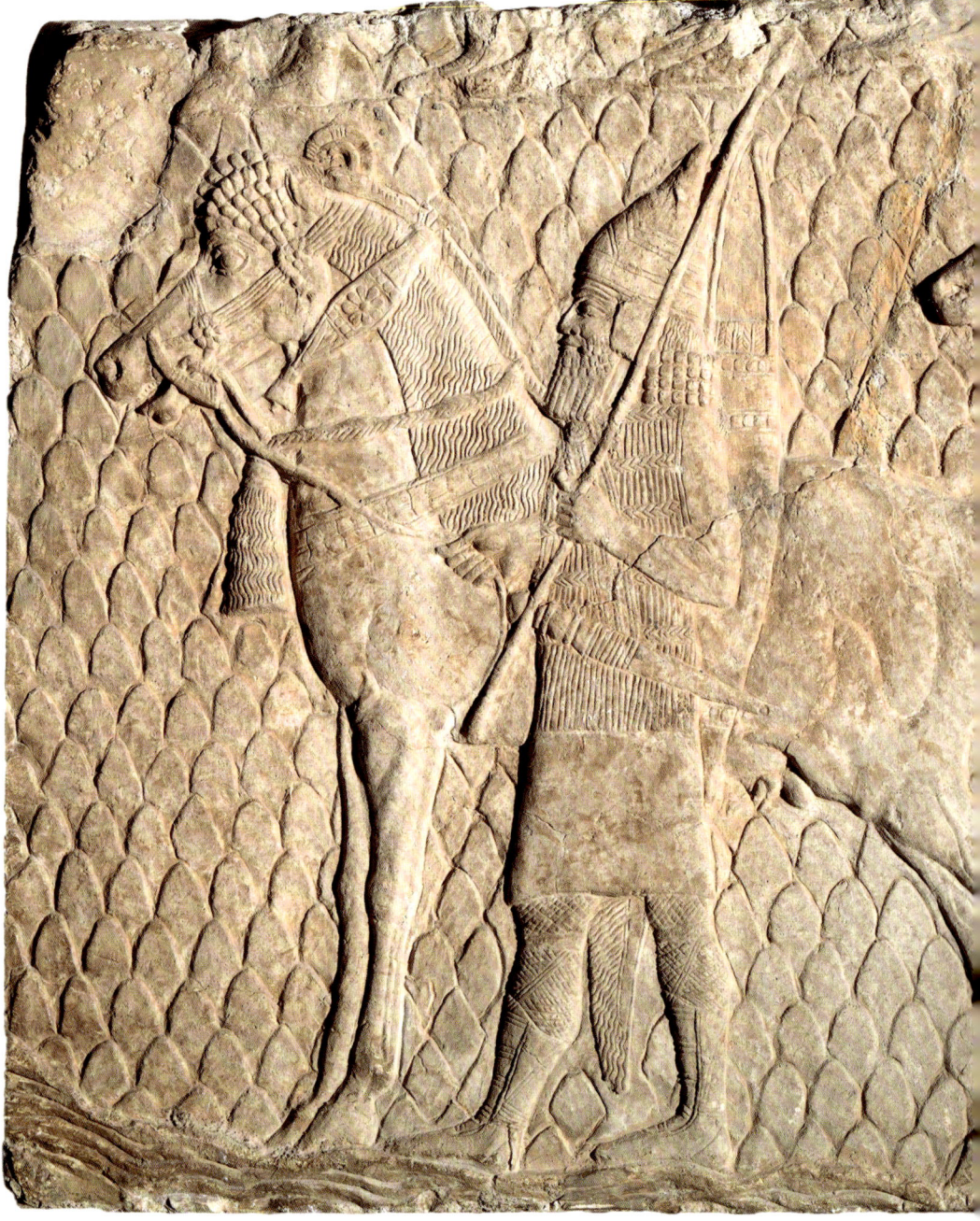

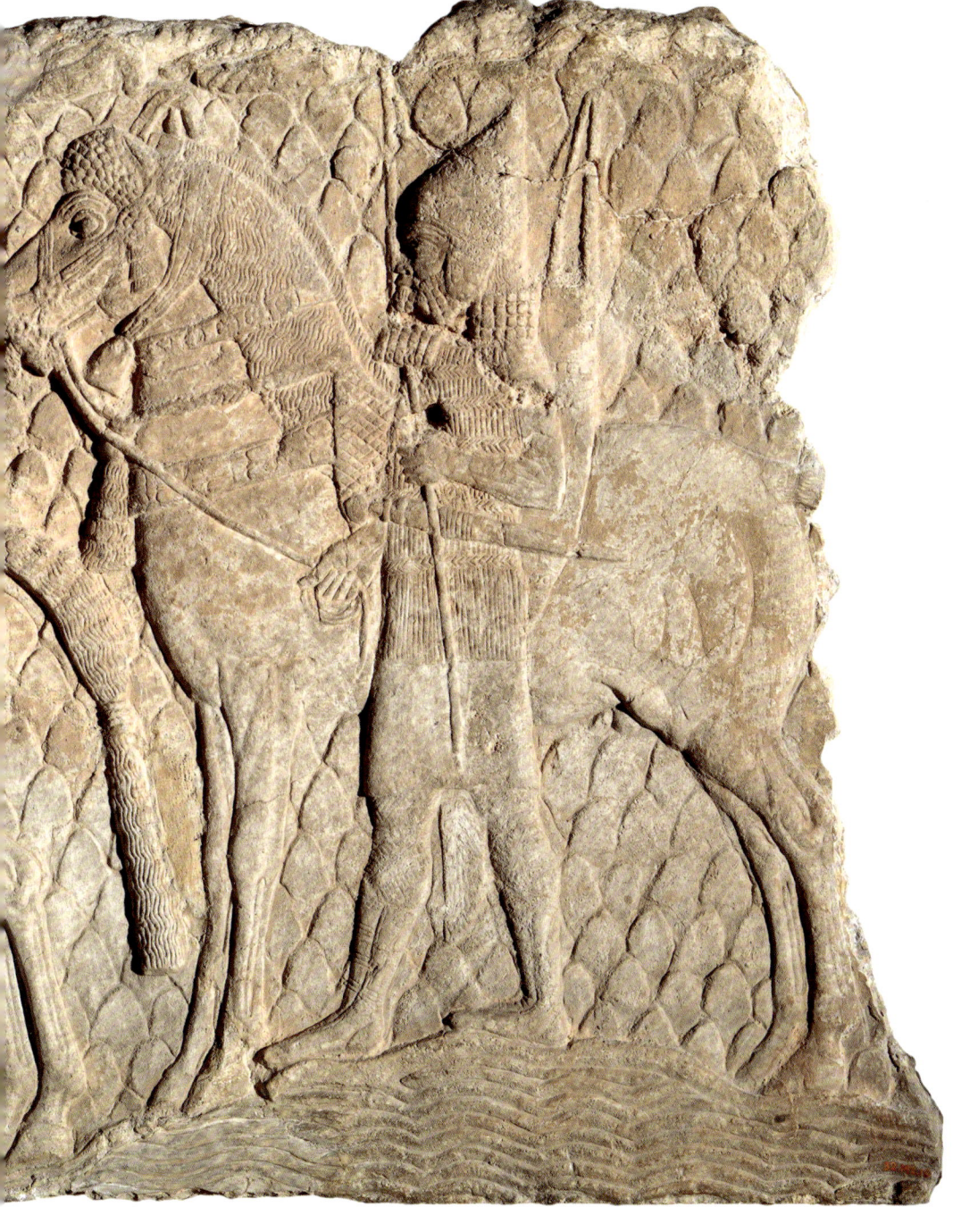

The history of the horse can be traced back fifty-five million years to the Eohippus, or 'Dawn Horse', which roamed Asia, Europe and North America. This timid, dog-sized creature evolved into the muscled modern horse we know today. Humans have similarly evolved, migrating from Africa to Asia around two million years ago and then eventually into Europe between about 130,000 and 115,000 years ago. Having first learned to use tools, our ancestors then developed language. As the cave paintings show, it was then not long before humans began creating visual art. Tellingly, the horse was there from the beginning.

The tradition of the horse in art reflects the connection between the horse and human in global history. Artists have illustrated this connection in charcoal on cave walls, oil paints on canvas, watercolour on paper, or as sculpture, installation and performance. The horse in art often holds up a mirror to our perception of humanity and society: across millennia, the figure of the horse has symbolised beauty, status, power, devastation, fragility, stagnation or progress, and much more. Communities dating as far back as the fourth millennium BCE in Kazakhstan, Ukraine and other parts of Eurasia depended on horses for their survival and prosperity: horse meat and milk from mares provided them with sustenance, while hides provided material for clothing and shoes. Sinews were used for thread and bones for utensils, tools and ornamentation. Over the next three millennia, horses spread throughout Europe and the Middle East. As horses increasingly became domesticated, horseback riding and the use of chariots resulted in humans travelling greater distances at speed.

Elsewhere, diverse cultures connected then clashed, leading to increased warfare with horses accompanying us into battle. The horse was crucial to the military campaigns of the Assyrians, skilled hunters and soldiers who lived in present-day Iraq and parts of Iran, Kuwait, Syria and Turkey. Assyrians kept records of the numbers of horses in their possession and whether they were suited to riding or draught work, both useful in combat. In a relief fragment from a palace decoration dating back to the

Bell-krater, late-fifth century BCE, terracotta, red-figure, 37.5 × 39.7

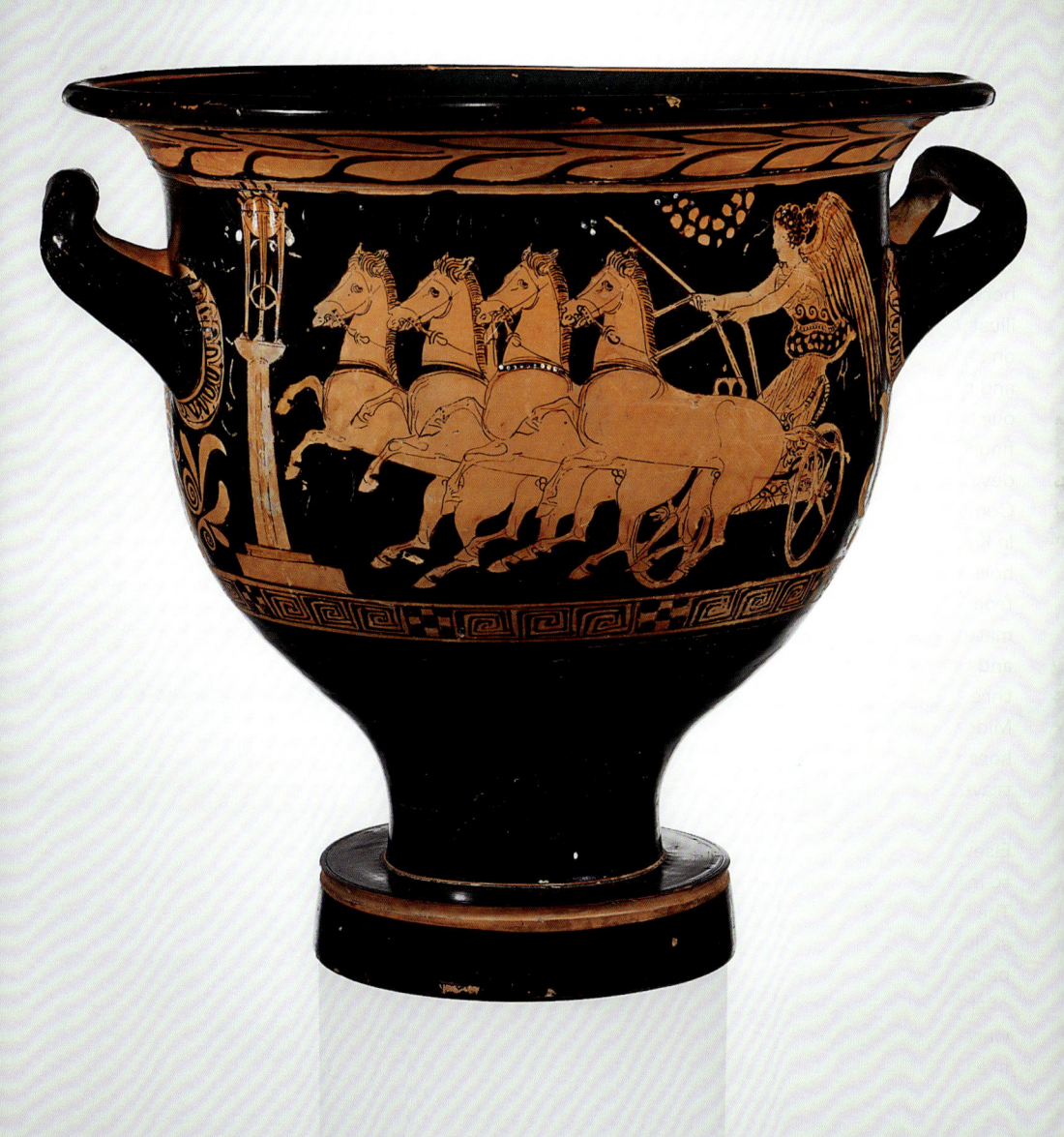

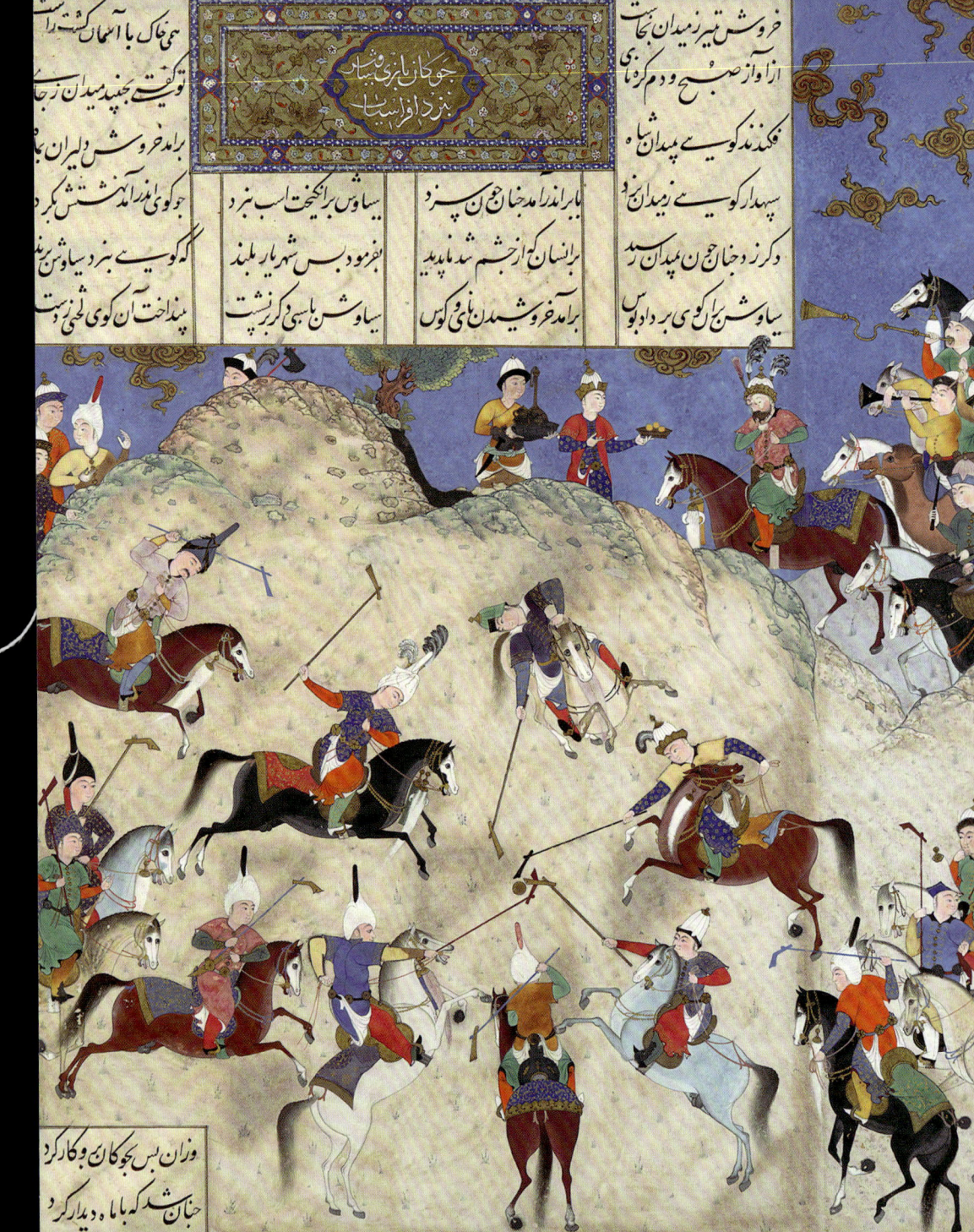

خروش تیبر زمیدان نجات

ازا وآزصبح ودم کرهای

فکند مدکوییے میدان شیا

سپهدار کوییے زیدان ه

دکرزوجهان جن من میدان زند

سیاوشن بے کوی مے برداد بوش

یاراندزامدجهان جوین سپرد

برلنان کم ارجشم شد ناپدید

برامد آخرخروشیمدن نای خی کوس

سیاوش برالختخ اسب نبرد

هفزمود بس شهریار بلبند

سیاوش باسپ فی کربنشت

بهی خاک با آسمان کشے رست

توکیسے بجهند میدان زجا

برامد خروش دلیران با

جوکوی ابرزامد آتش بکرد

کوییے نبزد سیاوش زند

بهداخت آن کوی لخی ز بہت

چوگان بازی بسیار
بنزد افراسیاب

وزان بس بچوگان وکارکرد

جهان شدکه بماه دیدارکرد

704–681 BCE reign of the Assyrian king Sennacherib, two horses are led along the bank of a river by two armoured soldiers (see p.9). The horses are richly harnessed; each wears a prominent tassel at neck height, embellished cheek pieces and a crest at the top of the head, suggesting the care, ceremony and reverence with which the Assyrian people treated their horses. They are shown standing still in the fragment, but the muscles finely carved into the alabaster hint at the speed and power that placed the horse at the centre of a formidable early Middle Eastern army and civilisation.

In Ancient Greece, horses were equally synonymous with conquest, victory and admiration in both war and sport. The Greeks introduced horse-racing to the ancient Olympic Games in the seventh century BCE. Spectators gathered to watch as four horses, yoked side by side, galloped at full speed around a hippodrome, pulling a chariot behind them. The horses and the chariot drivers – often hired professionals or enslaved people – navigated quick turns and gory collisions, requiring strength from the horse, skill in the driver and an instinctive bond between the two. The chaos of these chariot races would have been thrilling, and the energy of such a race is depicted on a terracotta bell-krater – a bowl for mixing wine and water – of the fifth century BCE which shows Nike, the winged goddess of victory, driving the four-horse chariot known as a quadriga (see p.11). The horses speed along the surface of the bowl, front legs elevated in a gallop. Nike and her formidable steeds are skilfully rendered with a fine brush against the glossy black background. This vase may have been made bespoke, or available to commemorate a victory.

The horse also takes a central sporting role in polo. Believed to have begun in Persia – now modern-day Iran – under the reign of Darius I (ruled 521–486 BCE), polo was generally played by the nobility. The small painting *Siyavush Plays Polo before Afrasiyab* c.1525–30 appears in the *Shahnama,* or 'Book of Kings', a poem narrating the history of the ancient kings of Iran, and illustrates the prestige and prowess associated with the sport.

Prince Siyavush commands a black horse in the middle of a field and at the centre of the picture, his plumed headdress is as ornate as the horse's trappings. Siyavush swings his mallet back, ready to free the ball from the riders swooping in dangerously close. The variously coloured steeds are likely the well-balanced Arab breed known for their endurance, athleticism, responsiveness to commands and agility in making quick turns and abrupt stops. The artist does not provide a faithful record of the sport, but spotlights the showmanship and display associated with it by setting the players against a sandy landscape and using a flattened perspective. From Persia, polo spread to Japan, China and India. It is there, in the nineteenth century, that the British encountered the sport. In both sixth century BCE Iran and twenty-first century Britain, polo and the horses associated with it connote the player's high social status and wealth. The horses are often Thoroughbreds or have a significant amount of Thoroughbred breeding, and their high pedigree echoes the lineage of British players who have historically and commonly had access to the game.

Concomitantly with war, conquest and sport, the horse was a vehicle for swift travel and communication. In the thirteenth century, Marco Polo (1254–1324) travelled to China to document the horse-centred messenger service of Kublai Khan (1215–1294), the Mongol ruler, founder and first emperor of the Yuan dynasty of China. Khan's grandfather, the tyrannical Genghis Khan, had ridden the Mongolian horse – a descendant of the Asiatic Wild Horse – on his notorious rampage across Asia, establishing one of the largest land empires in history. Marco Polo noted that at one point during Kublai Khan's rule, all roads of his empire were strategically punctuated by 10,000 horse posts each housing 400 horses, allowing riders to courier important news, such as the threat of an uprising, to the emperor with haste.

Communities once separated by distance were united by the horse under Kublai Khan. In the detail of a hanging scroll that was probably painted by the court painter Liu Guandao in 1280, Kublai Khan is dressed in white and sits on a black steed (right).

Yuan dynasty Liu Guandao, *Kublai Khan Hunting*, thirteenth century, hanging scroll, ink on silk, 182.9 × 104.1

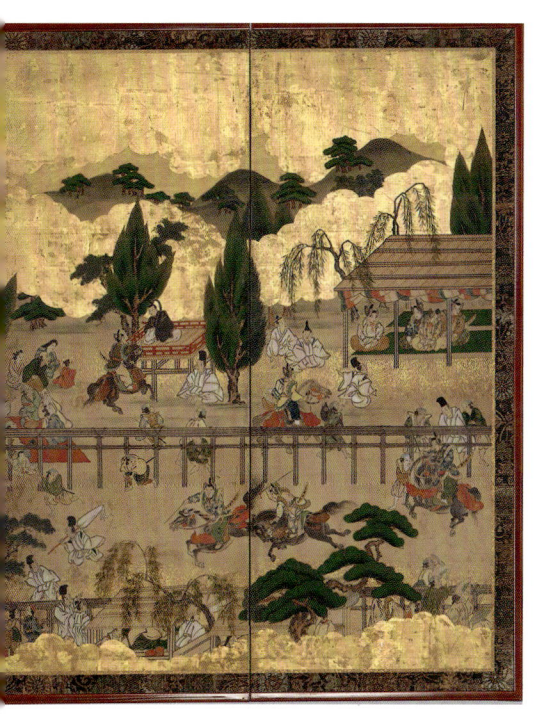

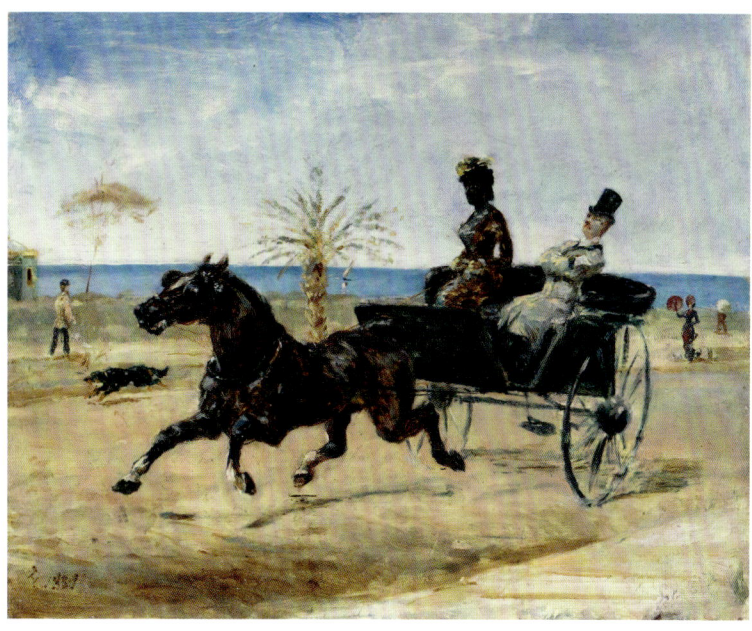

a two-wheeled carriage (see p.19). The rider on the right –
presumably the coachman, given his clothing – looks ahead
somewhat grumpily while his fellow passenger, believed to be
the Haitian aristocrat Anne Justine Angèle Delva de Dalmarie,
takes the reins. A small dog gives chase as the carriage tears
along Nice's shoreline. There is energy and a sense of the thrill
of speed in both these works.

Eighteenth-century British art of horses alone, without any
human presence, echo the images that our ancestors favoured
in the caves of Chauvet and Lascaux. George Stubbs (1724–1806),
one of the most celebrated artists of this period, found fame
as a painter of radically lifelike horses. In an unrelenting quest to
understand the physical make-up of horses, from the hide to the
muscles, arteries, sinews and down to the bone, Stubbs spent
eighteen months between 1756 and 1758 painstakingly dissecting
and drawing the bodies of horses at a remote farmhouse in
Lincolnshire, England, recording each layer of the horse's body
on drawings showing the front, side and back views (right). These
were then engraved onto eighteen plates – detailed, calm and
elegant images that mask the gore of Stubbs's project.

Whistlejacket c.1762, Stubbs's most famous painting, shows
a retired purebred Arabian chestnut racehorse almost life-size
against a plain background (overleaf). There is no reference to
a rider: the horse is dynamic and completely free. The textured
visible brushwork on the tail, a contrast to the smooth coat,
enhances the sense of Whistlejacket's movement. Though Stubbs
was knowledgeable about the anatomy of a horse and was usually
praised for his fidelity to nature, he exaggerated Whistlejacket's
rearing pose to create more drama and simultaneously show
more body parts than would naturally be visible. Given the size,
speed and power of horses, inaccurate poses were generally
overlooked in seventeenth- and eighteenth-century
representations; it was only with Edward Muybridge's *The Horse
in Motion* 1878, a series of sequential photographs showing the
movement of a horse in different stages of its gallop, that horse
postures previously invisible to the eye became visible.

George Stubbs, *The Anatomy of the Horse, including a particular
description of the bones, cartilages, muscles, fascias, ligaments, nerves,
arteries, veins, and glands* 1766, etching and graphite, 46.4 × 58.4

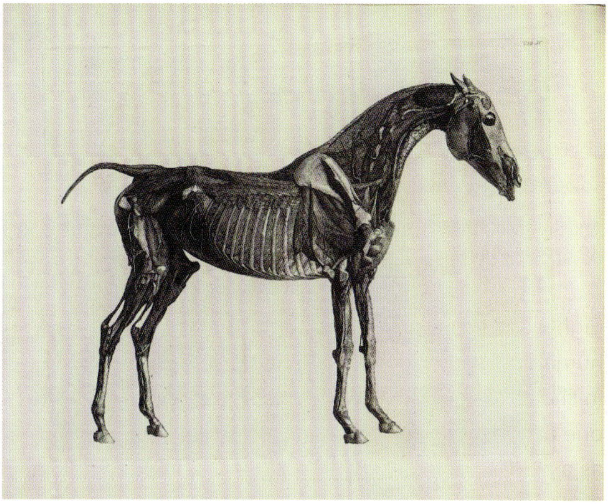

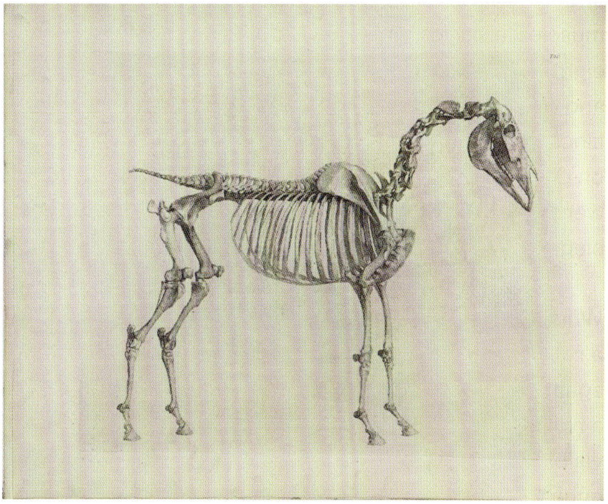

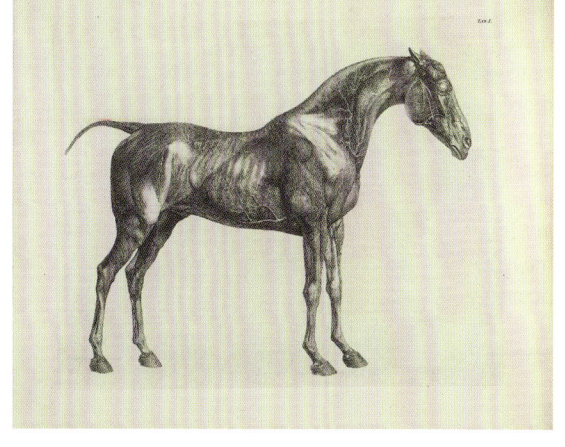

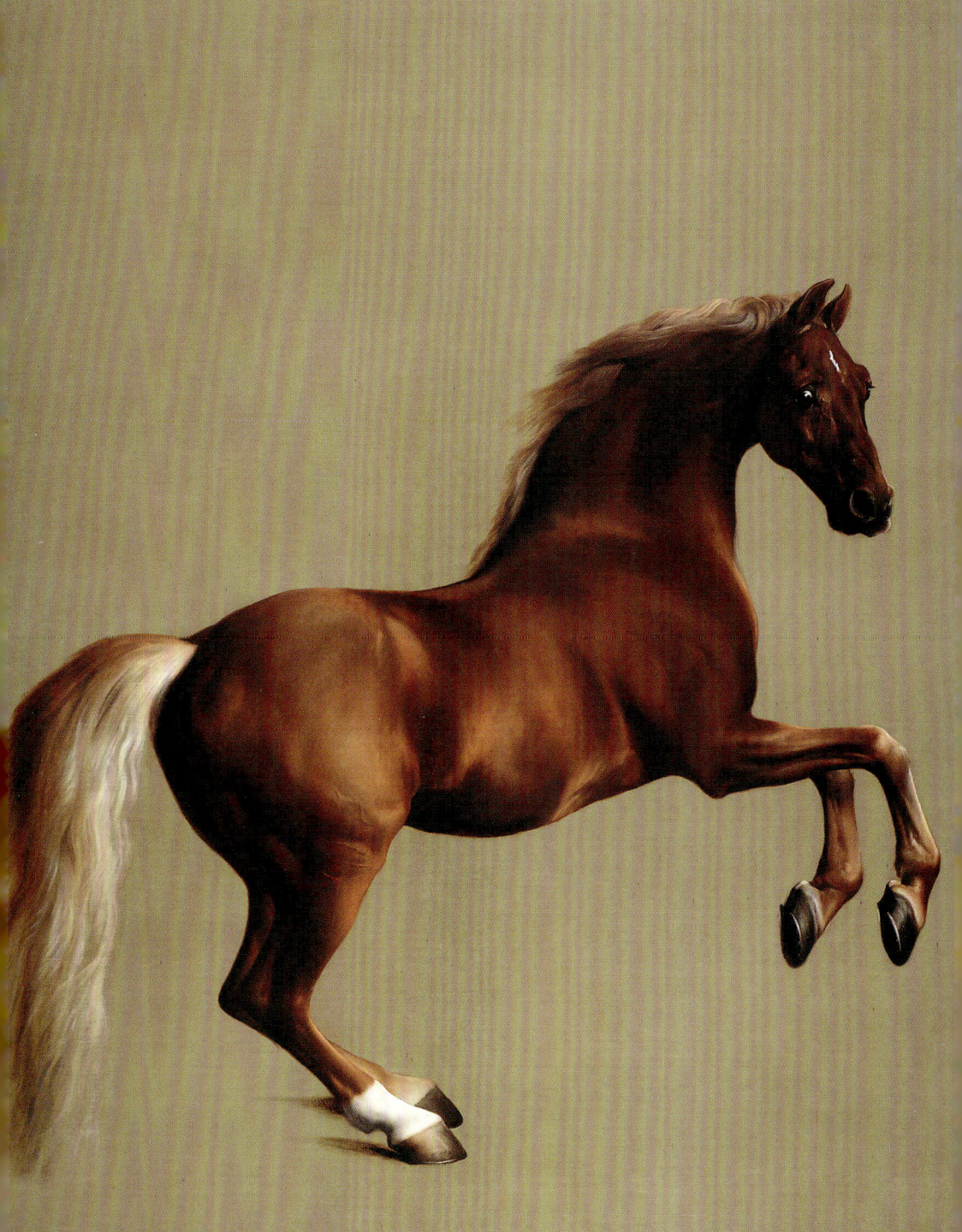

The longstanding close relationship between horse and human has inspired myriad artists to grapple with its various roles and meanings, up to the modern day. In *Equestrian Portrait of King Philip II (Michael Jackson)* 2010, Kehinde Wiley restages Peter Paul Rubens's c.1630 painting of Philip II of Spain, replacing the original's seventeenth-century monarch with Michael Jackson. The muscled steed, with exaggeratedly flowing hair and mane, gracefully performs a dressage move, while the iconic performer sits confidently atop it, dressed in elaborate armour and a voluminous cloak. In the twenty-first century, depictions of horse and rider that show both as powerful and graceful continue to abound, from Marina Abramović's film *The Hero* 2001 to the artwork accompanying Beyoncé's records *Renaissance* (2022) and *Cowboy Carter* (2024).

The following pages illustrate just a small segment of the global history of the horse in art, focusing on the depiction of horses from the mid-eighteenth century to today. These paintings, drawings, prints, sculptures and documented performances – all taken from the Tate collection – speak to British history and society, and were made by artists who were born, or have lived and worked in Britain. The artworks are organised thematically, exploring the resonances horses have at work, in conflict, for travel, at leisure, when racing or in mythology and literature. Historic and contemporary artworks sit side by side, showing that although horses have not featured prominently in everyday British life for about eight decades, their symbolism lingers in the human imagination.

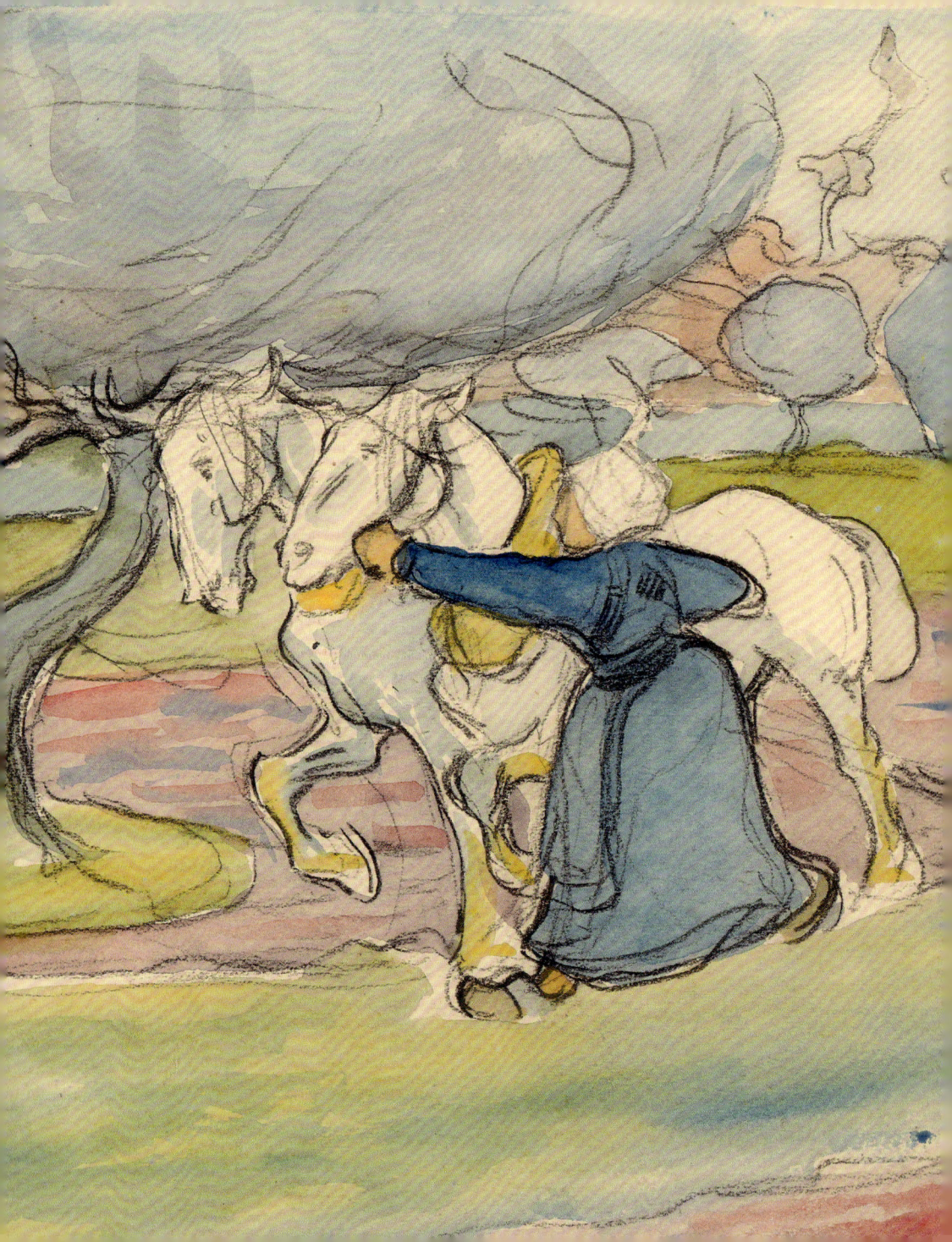

Work

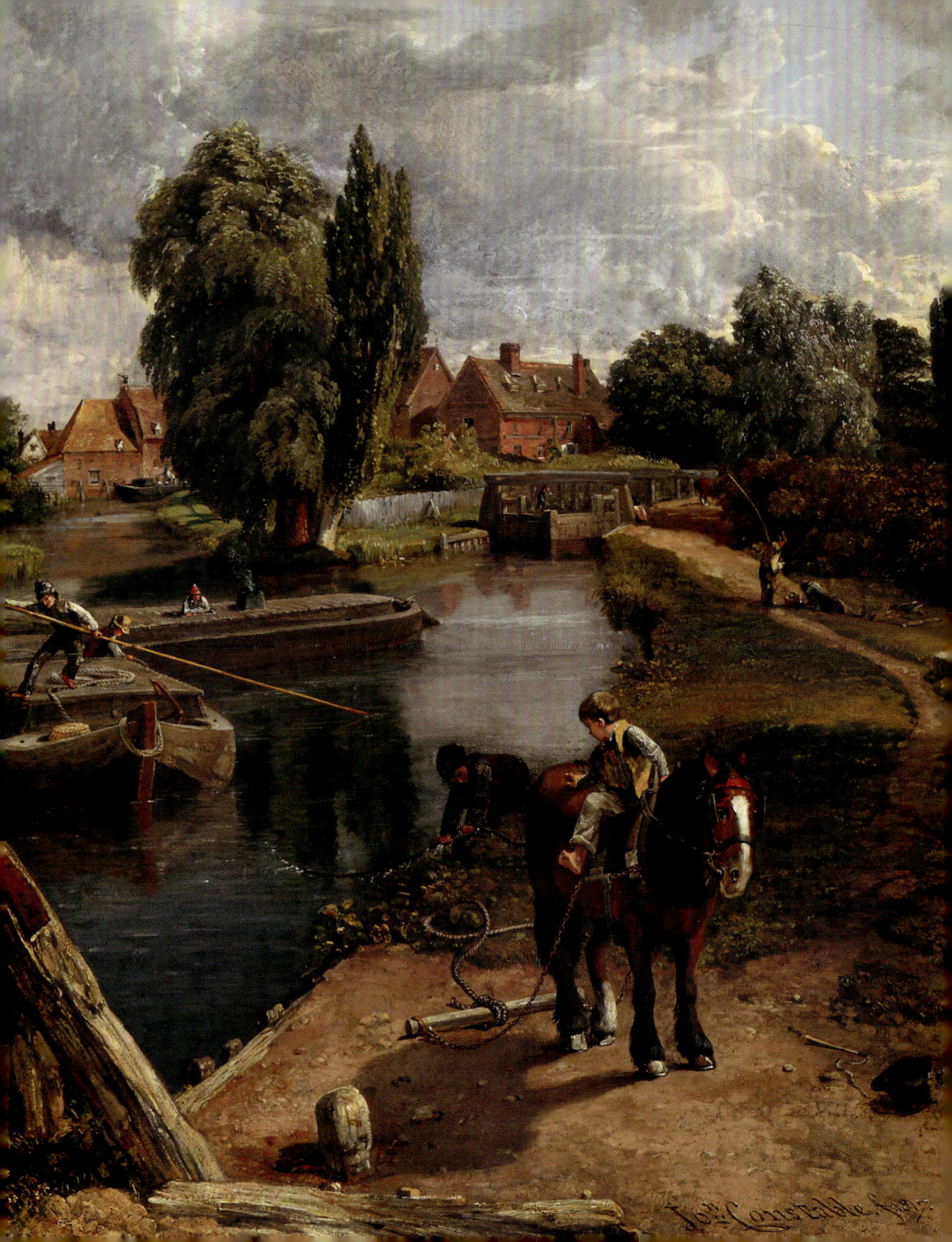

Horsepower and human endeavour frequently align in agriculture and industry. Scenes of eighteenth-century agricultural labour depict stocky draught breeds with broad backs and sturdy hindquarters carrying heavy loads and machinery at a time of considerable agricultural innovation. These horses and the rural working class exist harmoniously in a bucolic countryside, sharing in the daily tasks of life, tending to the ground and to each other. The industrious work horse is depicted with as much attention and beauty as the athletic hunter or brave war charger, in turn glorifying the rural working class. While the immediate reading of images of the rural horse at work is one of a simple, idyllic country life, horses did not just feature in rustic settings. Within rapidly growing towns, they pulled delivery carts, private carriages and omnibuses, while the pit ponies of an increasingly industrial society lugged mountains of coal underground. The common day-to-day animal becomes an impressive steed partnering with humans. British artists have visualised the grit and collaboration of the working horse, confirming the esteem with which it has been held.

Edwin Henry Landseer 1802–73
Shoeing exhibited 1844
Oil paint on canvas 142.2 × 111.8

Landseer portrays 'Old Betty', a bay mare characterised by
a reddish-brown coat with typical black colouration on the
mane, tail, ear edges and lower legs. Betty's coat is sleek and
shiny, a contrast to the tufted mane on the donkey and the
unkempt fur of the drooling dog. Light shines through the open
barn door onto Betty's muscled back and hindquarters and
down to the farrier who is working in her service, bent double
fitting her shoes. Betty appears majestic, towering over the
group. Landseer, a painter known for his emotive portrayals
of horses, dogs and stags, and for the four bronze lions in
Trafalgar Square, uses texture, light and composition to
glorify the work horse.

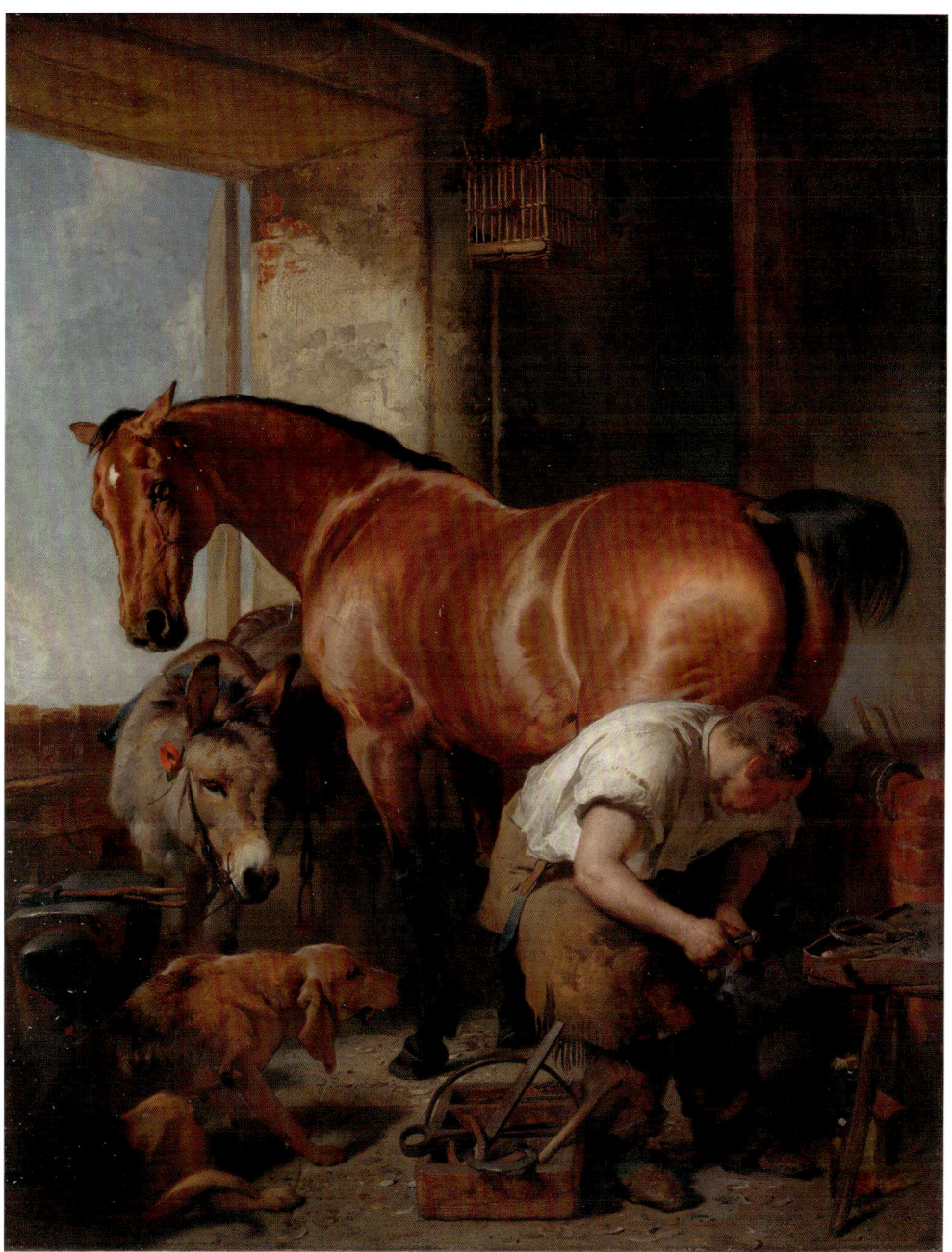

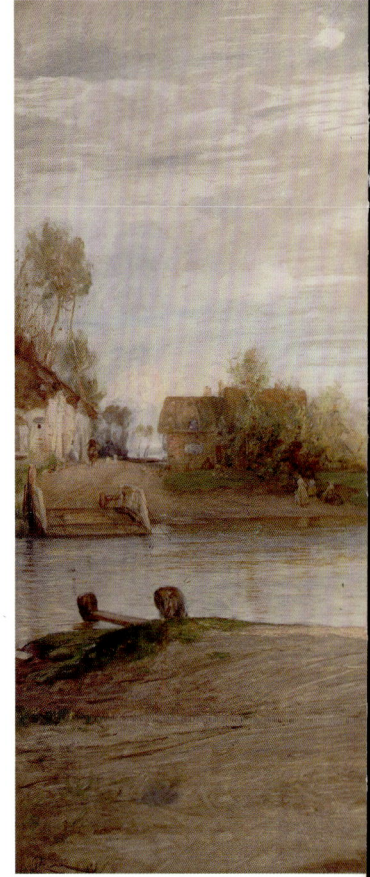

Robert Walker Macbeth 1848–1910
The Cast Shoe 1890
Oil paint on canvas 83.2 × 137.2

In Macbeth's rural scene, a smartly dressed man, perhaps
a local squire, leads a grey, nervous horse forward. Its big,
muscular frame and feathered feet suggest a solid and
dependable draft horse, while a docked tail was common for
working horses to prevent their tail being caught in a harness
or vehicle. There is no saddle for riding; the horse wears only
a bridle around its head and a surcingle – a leather strap
fastened around its girth using buckles. Perhaps it had been
pulling a wagon in a team and is now separated out to have
its shoe replaced. The aproned farrier waits before it, ready
to fit a new shoe.

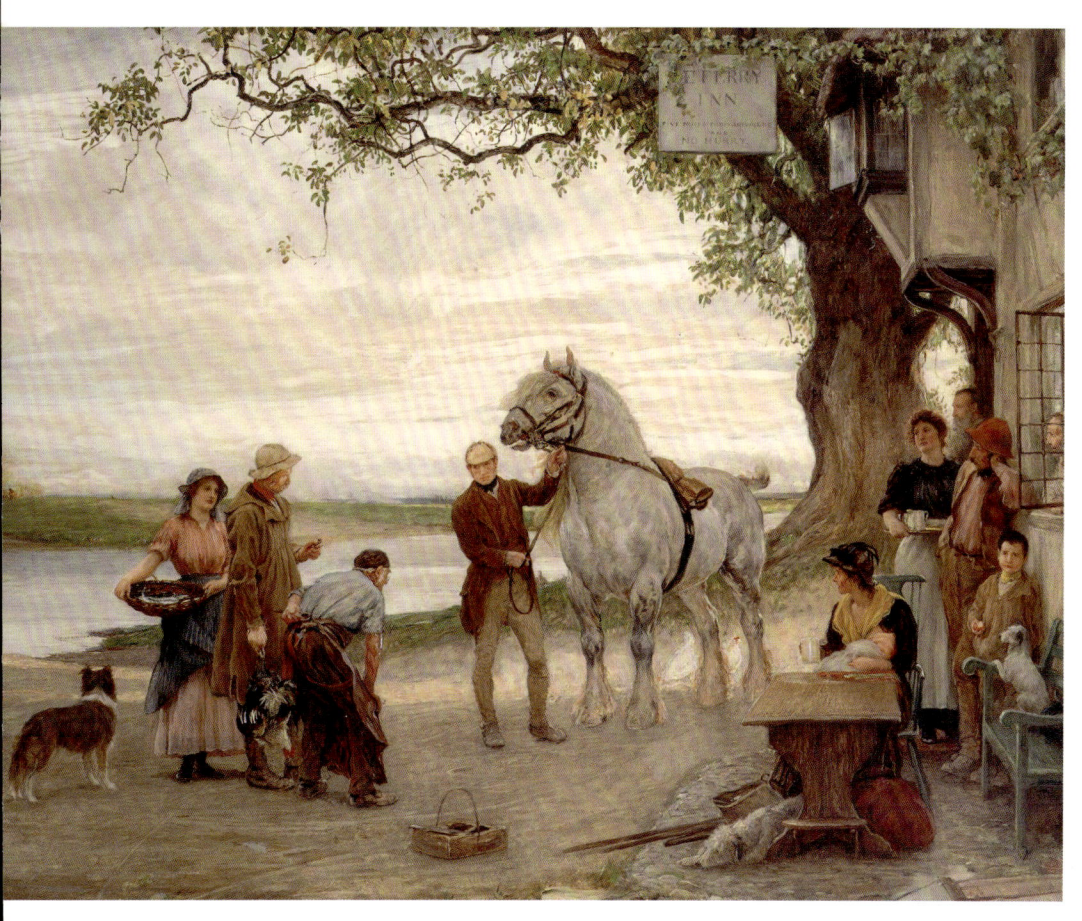

Robert Bevan 1865–1925
Ploughing in Brittany. Verso: Study of a Woman 1893
Conté crayon and watercolour on paper 25.6 × 35.2

A woman in traditional Breton dress leads two compact grey
plough horses through a field, followed by a male figure with
a wooden swing plough. The trees are still in leaf, suggesting
that the group is ploughing in the autumn. The horses are of
the Ardennes type, a heavy-boned and powerful draft breed
originally from Belgium, Luxembourg and France. It is likely
that the soil they are ploughing is soft, as only two horses are
required for the task. Bevan drew most of his image with Conté
crayon before applying watercolour in vivid shades of blue,
pink and green. Additional lines were added to emphasise the
rhythmic swirls and create a sense of harmony in the picture.

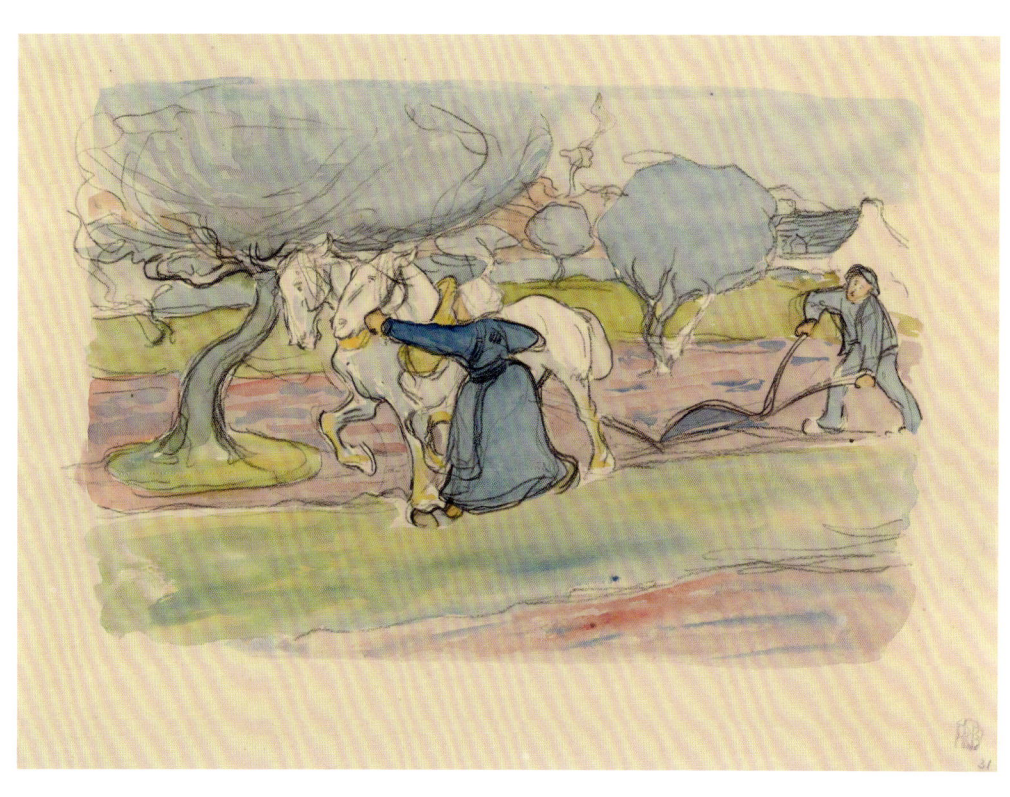

John Constable 1776–1837
Flatford Mill ('Scene on a Navigable River') 1816–17
Oil paint on canvas 101.6 × 127

In this painting a tow-horse with a white blaze down the middle
of its face stands still on the riverbank. The boy sitting astride
looks back at his companion who is releasing ropes so that
the barge it pulls can pass under Flatford Bridge to the left
of the picture outside the frame. Constable captures a moment
of working life at his merchant father's corn business. Horses
drew the barges between the family's watermills and dry dock.
Constable painted most of this scene on the spot while outside
but added the boy and the horse in the studio. X-rays show that
Constable initially painted another horse into the composition
on the towpath but replaced it with two boys.

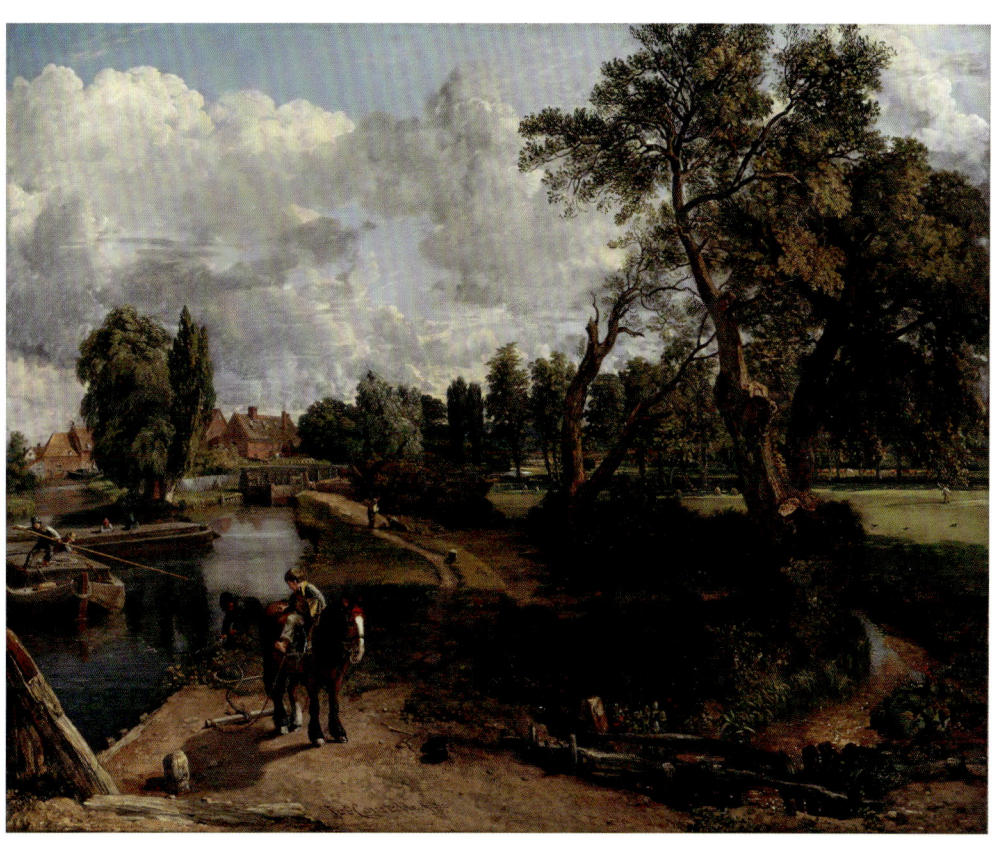

David Cox 1783–1859
Horse and Barge. Verso: tracing of horse from recto
Unknown date
Graphite and watercolour on paper 10.2 × 14

From the mid-eighteenth century, inland barges and boats
were pulled by donkeys, mules or smaller horse breeds. Cox's
watercolour on paper is a stylised, quick and abbreviated sketch
of such a working animal. The horse wears a plum-coloured collar
around its neck to help distribute the weight of the barge it is
pulling, while the brown bar behind its legs and under the tail is
where the barge is attached. A beige blanket, or quarter sheet,
covers the horse's rump to keep its muscles warm and supple
when working in cold weather. Cox depicts a feedbag attached
to the horse's head, his thin beige-grey brushstrokes making it
difficult to discern. Cox perhaps used this sketch as a study for
a more a finished watercolour.

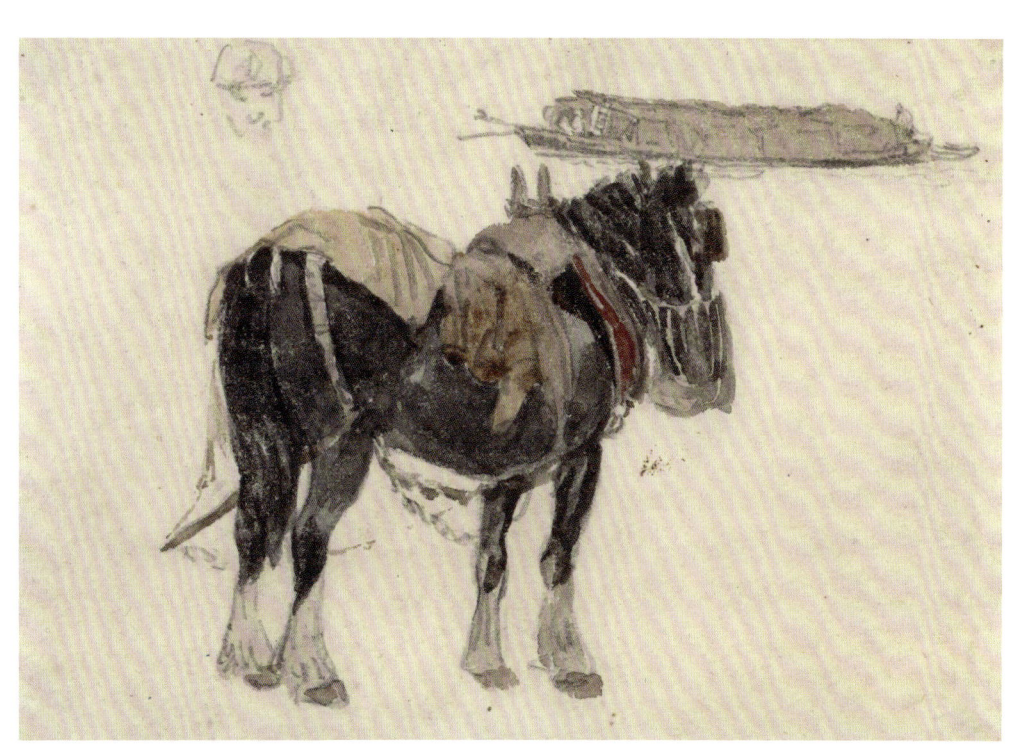

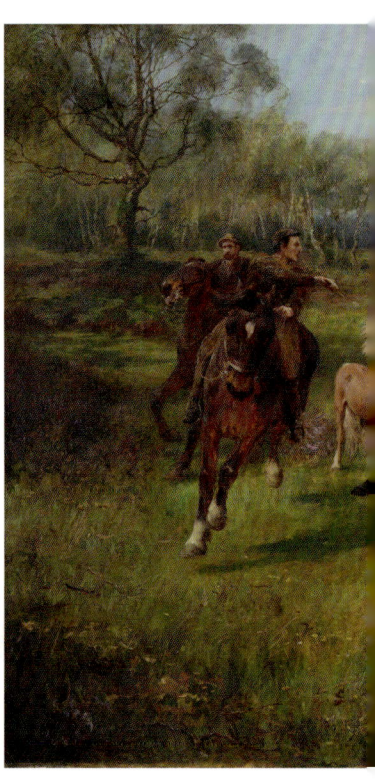

Lucy Kemp-Welch 1869–1958
Colt Hunting in the New Forest 1897
Oil paint on canvas 153.7 × 306

Measuring over three metres wide, Kemp-Welch's monumental
painting shows mounted riders hunting herds of free-roaming
ponies in the New Forest. They are at full gallop, several in
a moment of suspension with all four legs off the ground.
Some of the ponies – traditionally referred to as colts
irrespective of their age, gender and whether or not they are
castrated – will be sold to be employed in transportation,
agriculture, breeding and racing. The rest will be released back
into the open forest. New Forest ponies have inhabited the area
for approximately two thousand years, shaping the region's
ecosystem to what it is today: their grazing limits overgrowth
and facilitates the growth of rare plant species like chamomile
and pennyroyal mint.

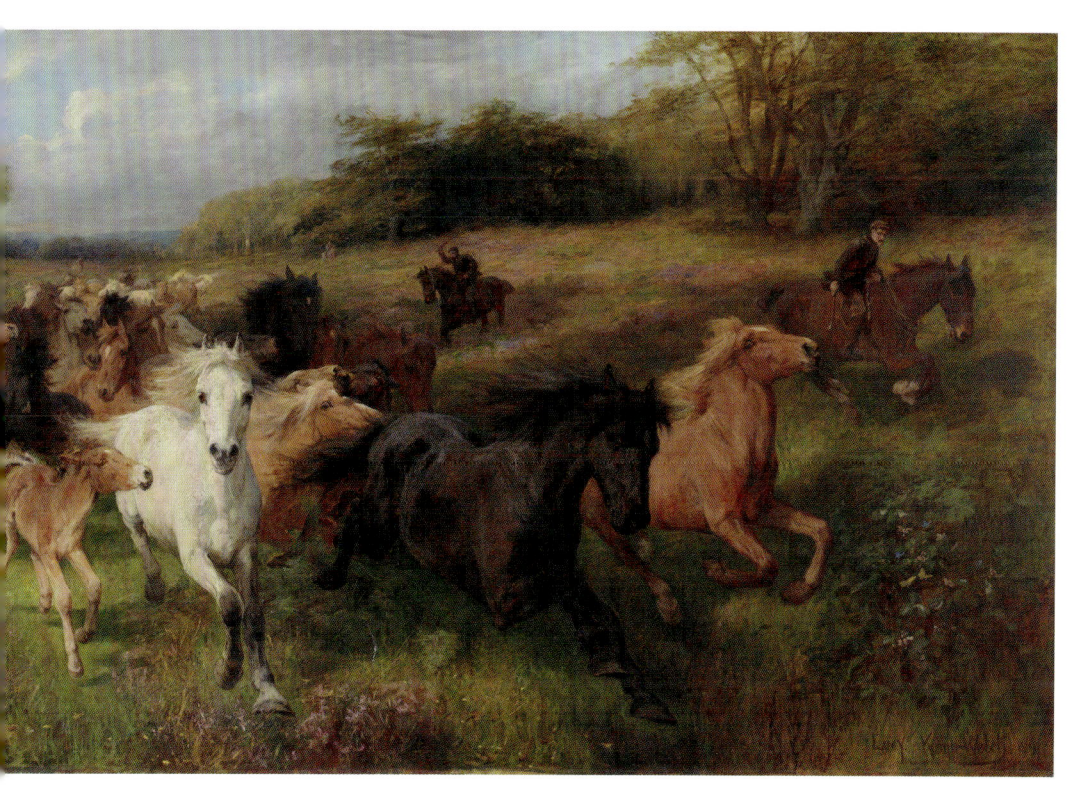

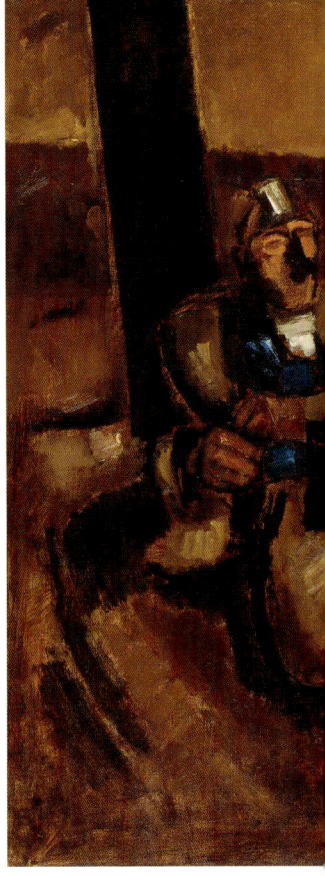

Josef Herman (1911–2000)
The Pit Pony 1958–9
Oil paint on canvas 111.8 × 185.4

At the centre of this frieze-like composition, a pit pony and
a coal miner stand side by side. They appear as though they are
one, a fusion of working man and working horse. Pit ponies
powered machinery and transported coal to the surface and to
the customer. It is not clear whether Herman's miners and pony
are underground or outside. His palette is dominated by an
earthy brown, further emphasising this merging of man, horse
and nature. Herman's stylisation of the miners and pony is
distinct and confident. Neither the workers nor the pony have
individualising features, yet they are statuesque on a canvas
that measures just under two metres wide. Herman depicts
them as heroic in their everyday lives as labourers.

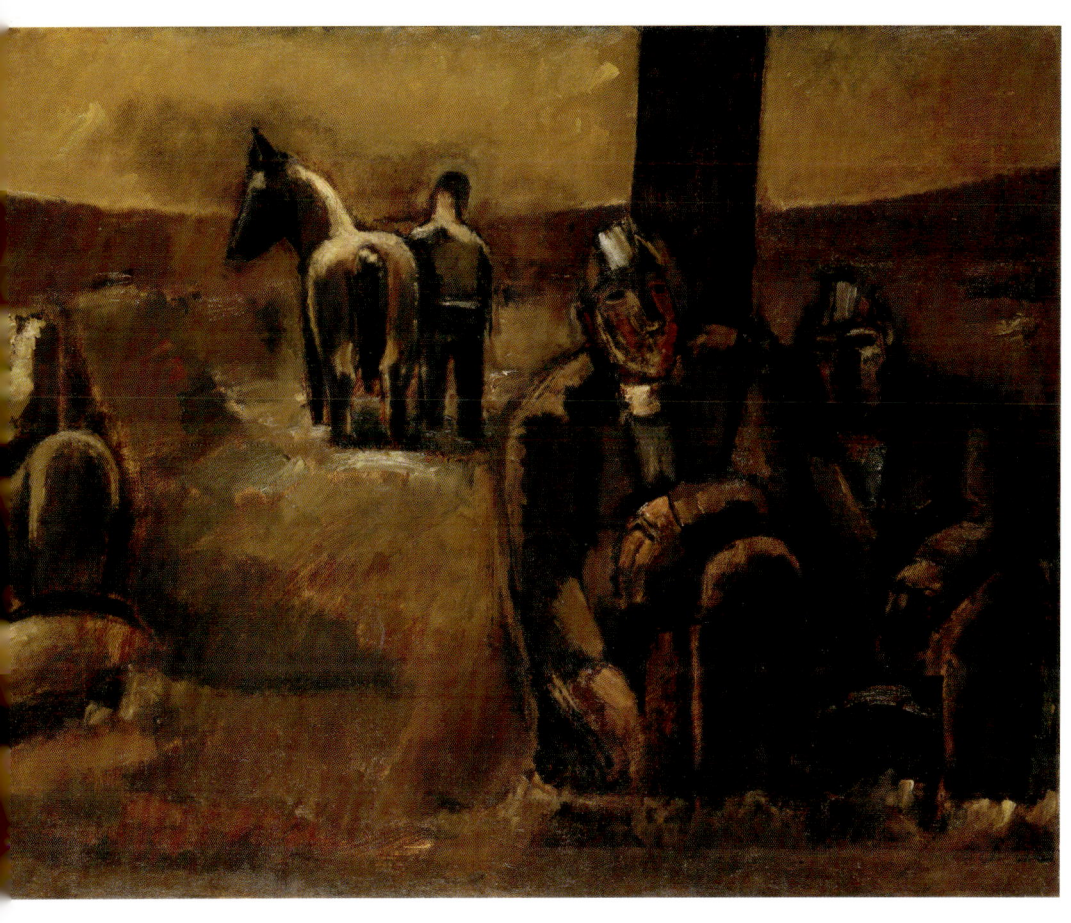

Tania Bruguera born 1968
Tatlin's Whisper #5 2008
Performance, two people and two horses

Tatlin's Whisper #5 was an unannounced performance staged
by Tania Bruguera at Tate Modern one weekend in 2008, in which
riders who appeared to be members of London's Metropolitan
Police Mounted Branch exercised crowd control techniques
on museum visitors who happened to be present. The horses
became agents of authority alongside their human riders,
using their height advantage and greater body mass to push
audiences forward, encircle groups to make them tighter, or
break up the audience into smaller groups. Without context,
the audience was herded around the Turbine Hall, inducing
feelings of confusion and even fear. The title refers to Russian,
Ukrainian and Soviet artist Vladimir Tatlin (1885–1953) who
employed his art and architecture to critique Soviet
propaganda. Bruguera's performances use silence and self-
censorship to both implement and resist power structures.

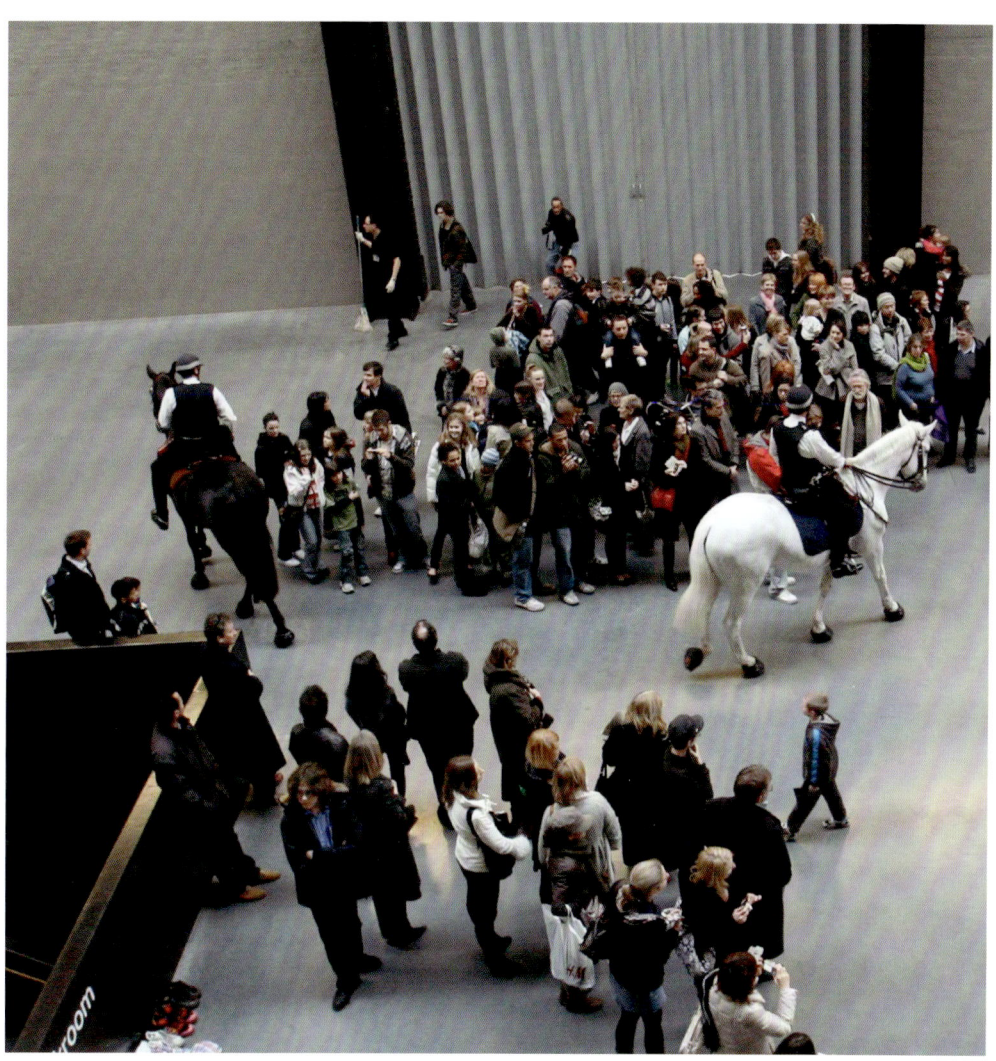

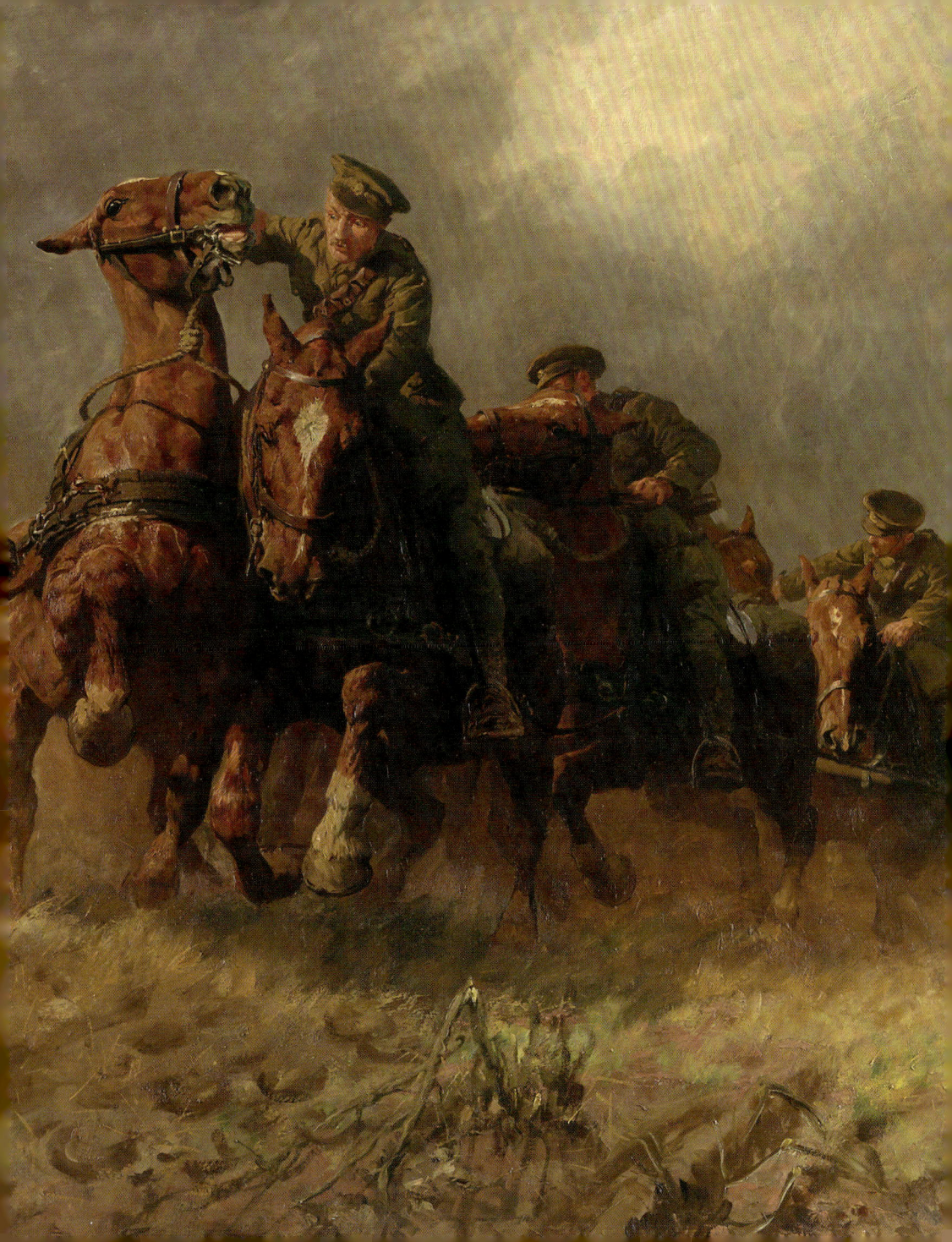

Conflict

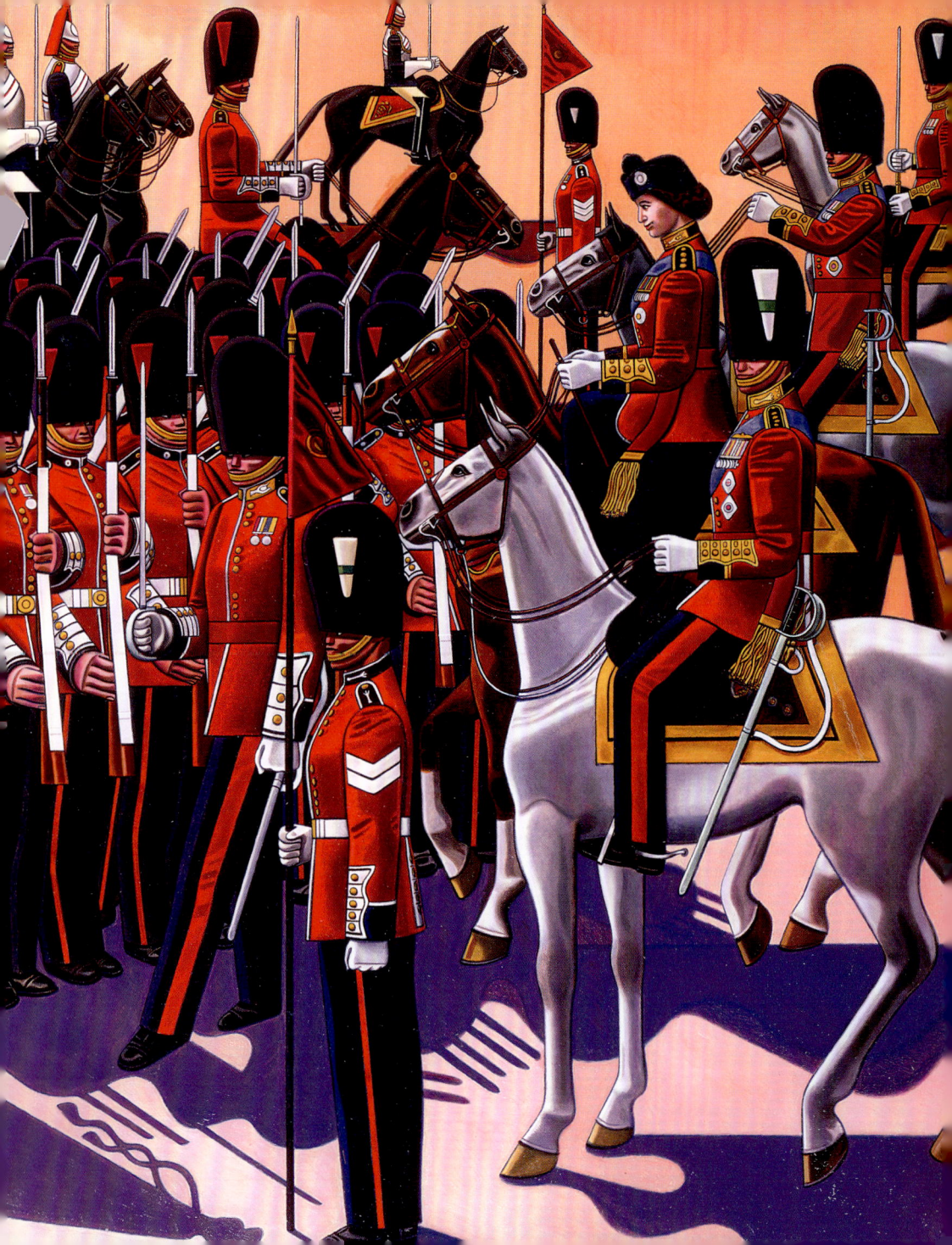

Globally, horses have been our comrades-in-arms, steadfast in the subjugation of lands and the amassing of power – but also a means of resisting these forces. Equine imagery in a martial context represents their function in mounted charges, reconnaissance, safe withdrawal and hauling supplies, but also their symbolic associations. Units of horses thundering forward bring a sense of ferocity to a battle scene and show its scale. Military men in armour and uniform alone are impressive, but become even more powerful pictured astride a spirited and muscled steed, with the depiction of a powerful, agile, brave and well-trained creature implying that the rider, too, possesses these characteristics. Artistic inspiration is found in this valiant soldier and steed at war, but also in glory turned to futility and waste, with displays of fear and fatigue in a remarkable creature amplifying the turmoil associated with war. Honest portrayals of the cost to the horse of charging into battle and ensuring a soldier's survival elicit reflection. In contemporary visual culture, ceremonial processions and the commemoration of these military horses recall a nation's military might.

Joshua Reynolds 1723–92
Lord Ligonier 1760
Oil paint on canvas 281.2 × 235.7

In this whole-length portrait, military officer Lord Ligonier is
shown on horseback. In the background on the left is a fortress
and on the right are soldiers in battle. Ligonier appears calm
on the fiery steed: neither soldier nor horse shows any sign of
discouragement. Ligonier wears the blue uniform of the Royal
Horse Guards, a cavalry regiment of the British Army that favours
Irish Draught horses. His horse is a bay with two white socks
on the hind legs and is of the impressive stature characteristic
of Irish Draughts. The elaborate trappings on the horse are
typical for men of Ligonier's rank: the bit on the horse's chest
is decorated with half-moons and his tasselled saddle cloth is
heavily embellished.

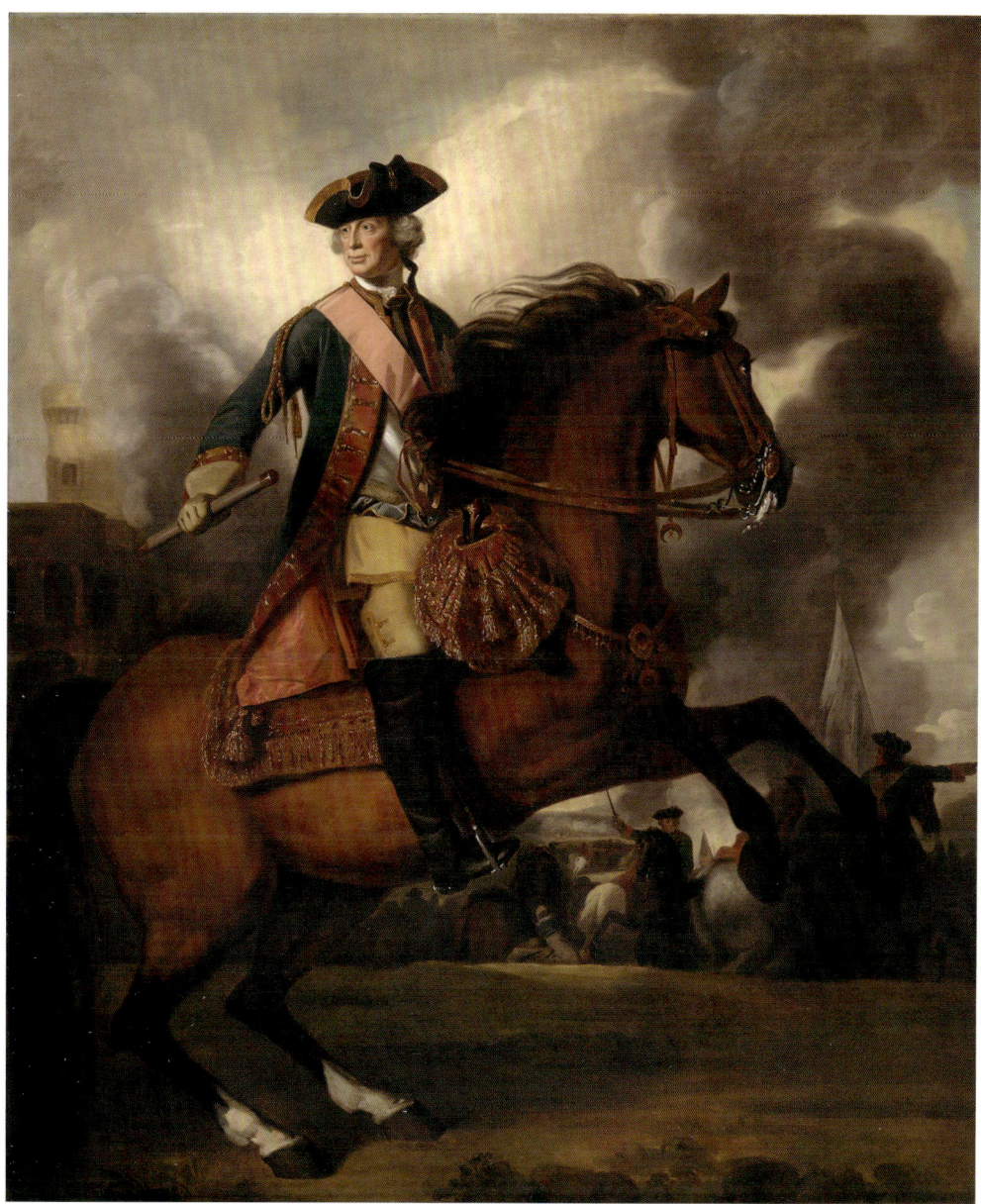

Samuel Waller 1850 1903
Sweethearts and Wives 1882
Oil paint on canvas 144.8 × 201.9

A group of armed and armoured men on horseback return
to the safety of their castle and the joyous welcome of their
sweethearts and wives. They are moss-troopers, raiders who
operated in the marshy lands between Scotland and England in
the seventeenth century, plundering livestock indiscriminately
from both sides. Waller depicts small, surefooted horses that
were likely capable of moving through swampy ground and
clambering up mountains in the dark or in terrible weather.
The three horses at the front of the group are meticulously
painted, demonstrating Waller's skill as a painter both
of animals and genre scenes; depictions of everyday lives. The
full assembly of horses and riders are seen through the gate,
Waller's use of fading emphasising their great number.

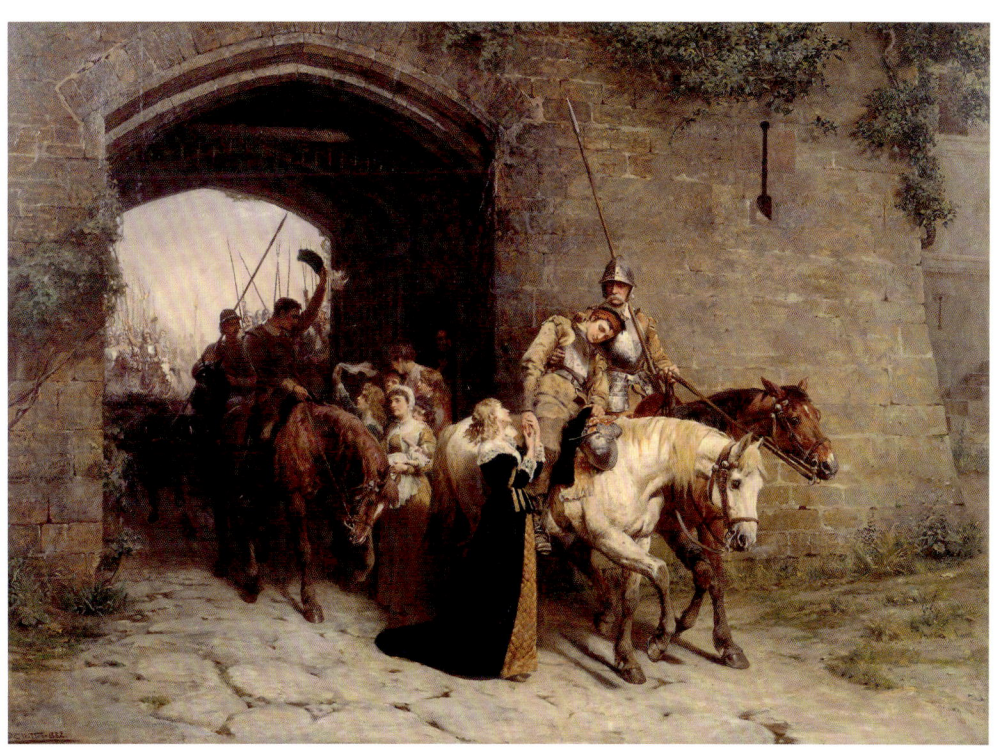

Samuel Waller 1850–1903
Success! 1881
Oil paint on canvas 134.6 × 213.4

In the aftermath of a duel, the young victor is accompanied back to his horse-drawn carriage. His unfortunate opponent is dragged off the field in the distance. Neither of these two men occupy the central position in Waller's composition, however, nor are they large in scale: instead, it is the horse and carriage that dominates the painting. Two bays lead the group, with two chestnuts in the rear, the coats of all four glistening and their muscles rippling. The near horses are saddled, and a postilion rider is slouched on the back of one. In one hand he grips the reins and in the other a whip, demonstrating the control needed over the athletic horses – yet his pose betrays a sense of arrogance and recklessness, perhaps a comment on the imprudent nature of settling personal vendettas in this manner.

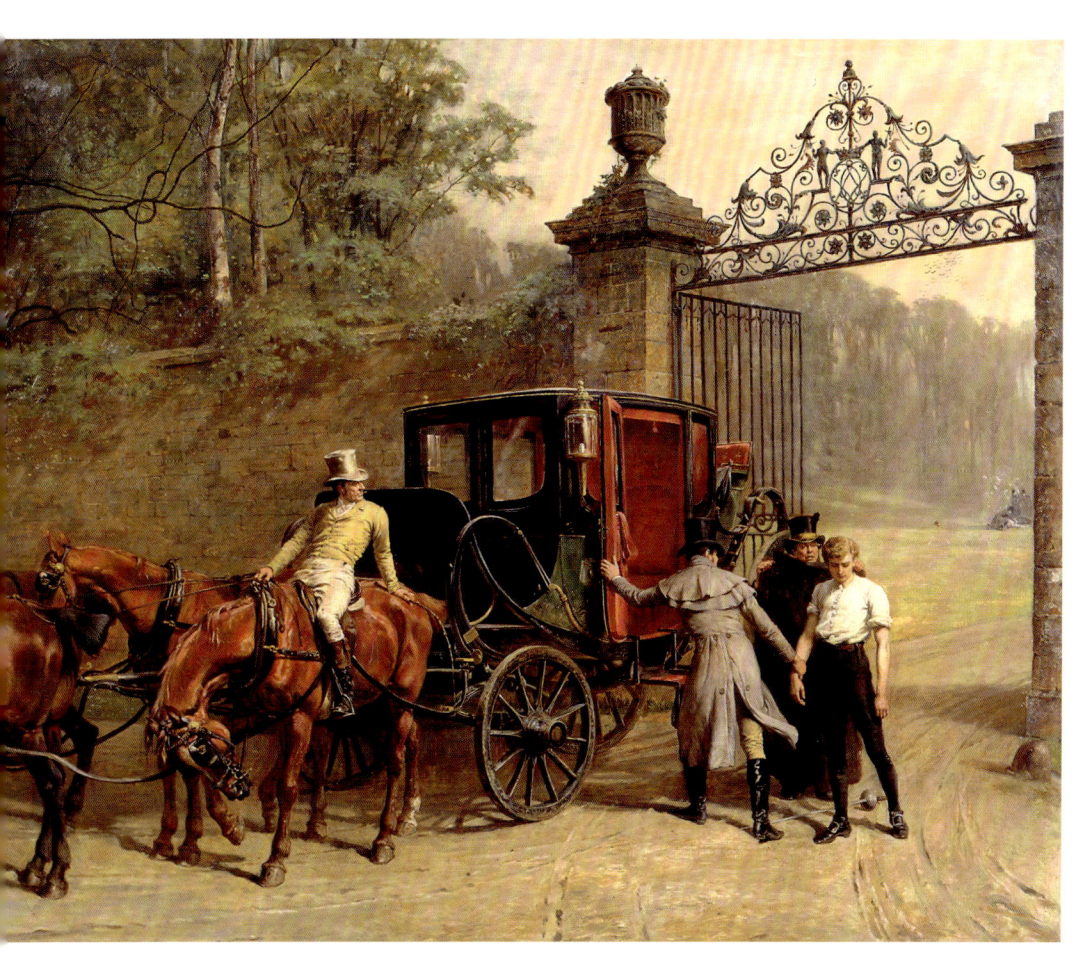

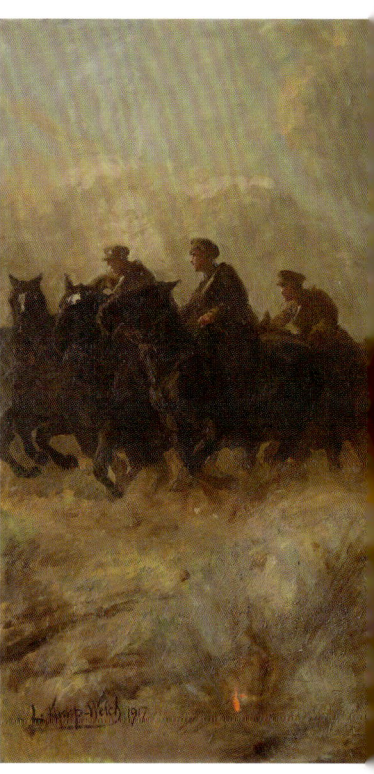

Lucy Kemp-Welch 1869–1958
Forward the Guns! 1917
Oil paint on canvas 152.4 × 306.1

Teams of horses, yoked in three pairs, charge towards the
viewer, the might of their hooves loosening the ground beneath
them. They are being trained on Salisbury Plain, southern
England, for military service in the First World War. A soldier
sits on the horse on the left of each pair, controlling both
horses. The cart pulled by the central group is obscured, but
from the title of Kemp-Welch's painting we are to imagine a field
gun. For heavier field artillery like howitzer guns, as many as
ten horse pairs were required. Kemp-Welch, the leading horse
painter of her time, painted this image from sketches made on
Salisbury Plain. Soldiers repeatedly drove the horses towards
her while she stood behind her easel capturing the general
outline of their movement.

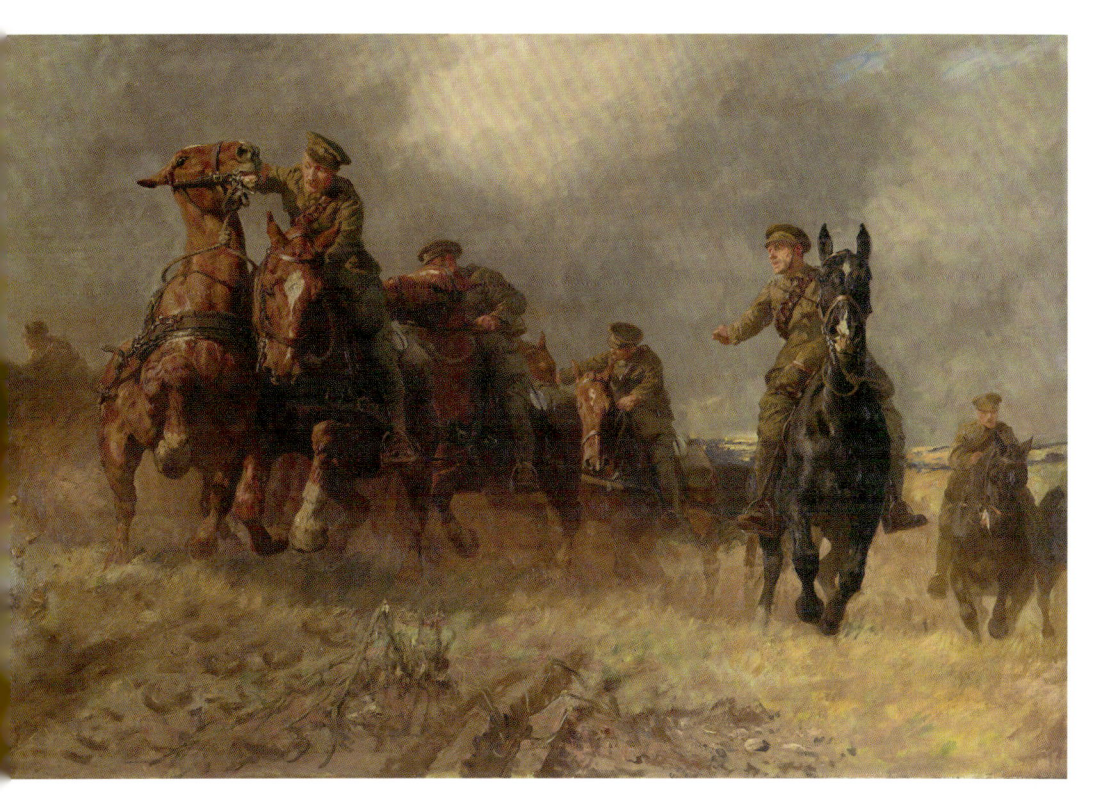

Elizabeth Butler (Lady Butler) 1846–1933
The Remnants of an Army 1879
Oil paint on canvas 132.1 × 233.7

The Remnants of an Army, painted during the Second Afghan War (1878–80), depicts the defeat of the British in the First Afghan War (1839–42). Lady Butler's largest painting shows army surgeon William Brydon slumped in the back of the saddle as he turns to face the rescue party arriving on horseback from the British fort at Jalalabad. It is only the determination of his exhausted chestnut, clambering along the last rocky stretch before the fort, that carries them forward. Lady Butler wrote that she 'never painted for the glory of the war, but to portray its pathos and heroism.' The horse's buckling knees, bloodshot eyes and parched tongue elicit emotions of sympathy and sorrow while evoking its bravery. Brydon survived the ordeal, but his horse did not recover.

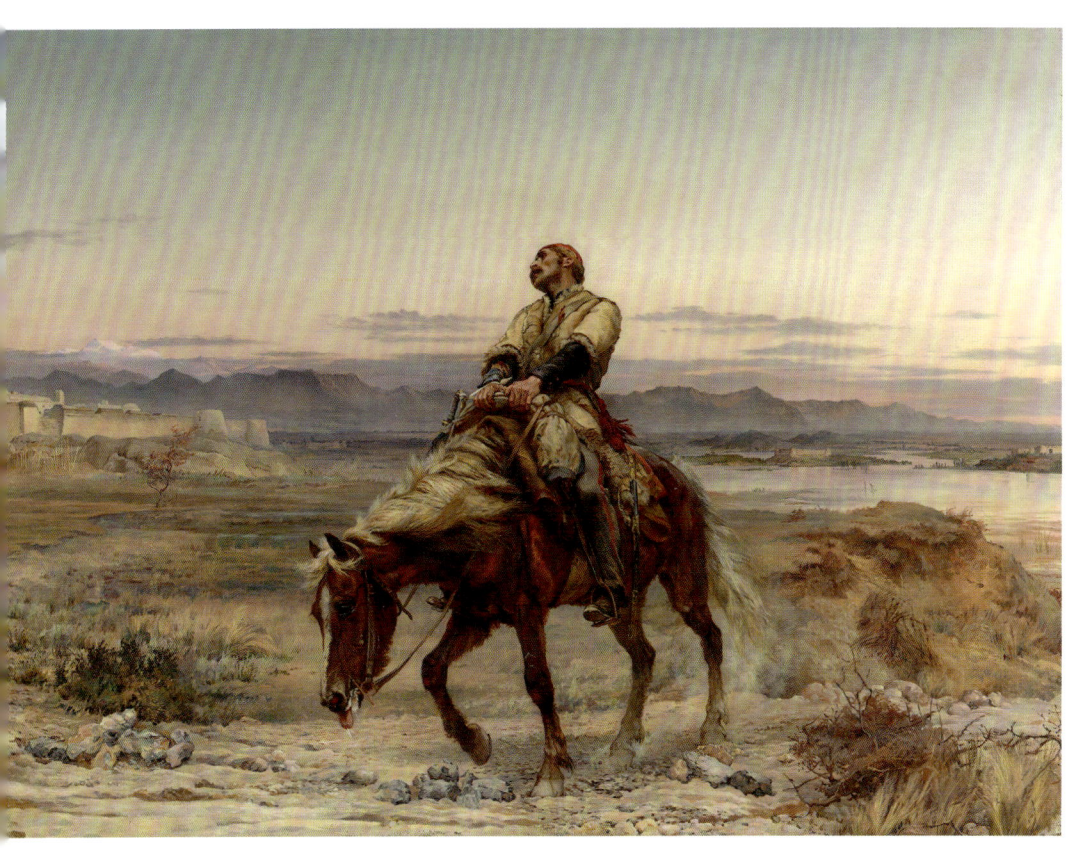

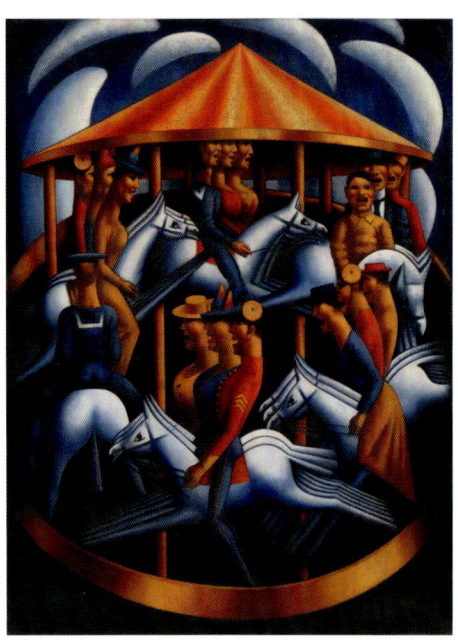

Mark Gertler 1891–1939
Merry-Go-Round 1916
Oil paint on canvas 189.2 × 142.2

Men and women in both civilian clothing and military uniform
sit stiffly on a carousel of horses, their mouths open in a silent
cry in unison. The ghostly horses, teeth bared, appear just as
agitated. All associations with enjoyment are stripped off the
children's amusement ride: the carousel, now a metaphor for
the relentless military machine, circles round and round with
no end in sight. Both horses and humans are trapped. Gertler's
muted palette, dominated by dark blue, and the dizzying tilt
of the carousel heighten the sense of horror in the scene.
Gertler painted *Merry-Go-Round* during the First World War
while living in London as a conscientious objector.

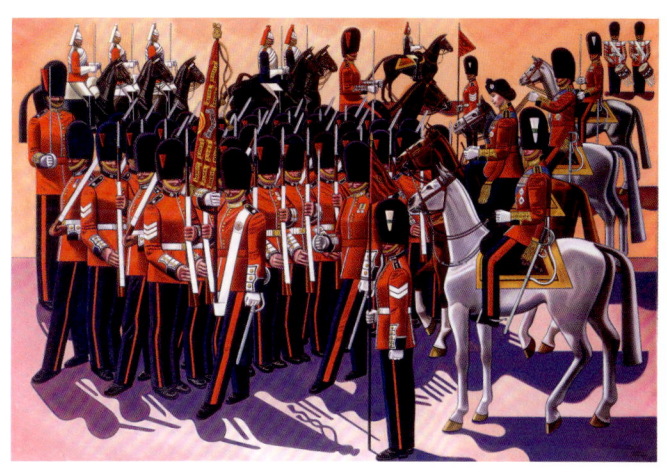

William Roberts 1895–1980
Trooping the Colour 1958–9
Oil paint on canvas 182.9 × 274.3

Queen Elizabeth II, wearing a small black cap, sits on a chestnut on the right-hand side of the painting, with her husband the Duke of Edinburgh to her left as they attend Trooping the Colour, a ceremonial event performed every year in London to celebrate the birthday of the reigning monarch. A 'colour' refers to the regimental flag that is carried by different units. The soldier walking diagonally at the front of the group to the left holds a colour naming famous battles in British history, at whose centre is the motto 'En Ferus Hostis' (Behold a Fierce Enemy). Horses surround the group, alert and poised, forming part of this bold and fierce enemy. Two of them carry the head of state and her husband, further associating their symbolism with power and importance.

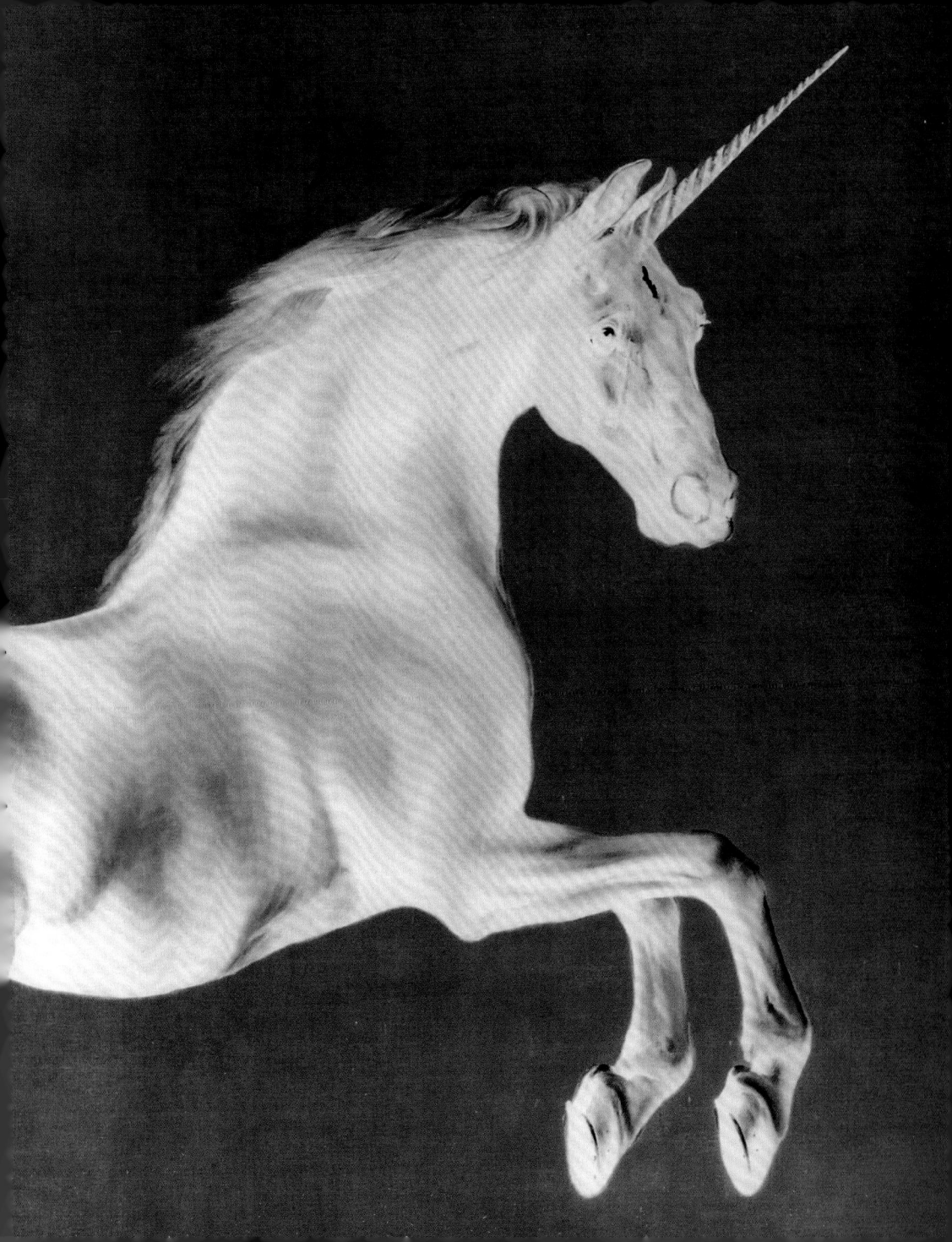

Mythology

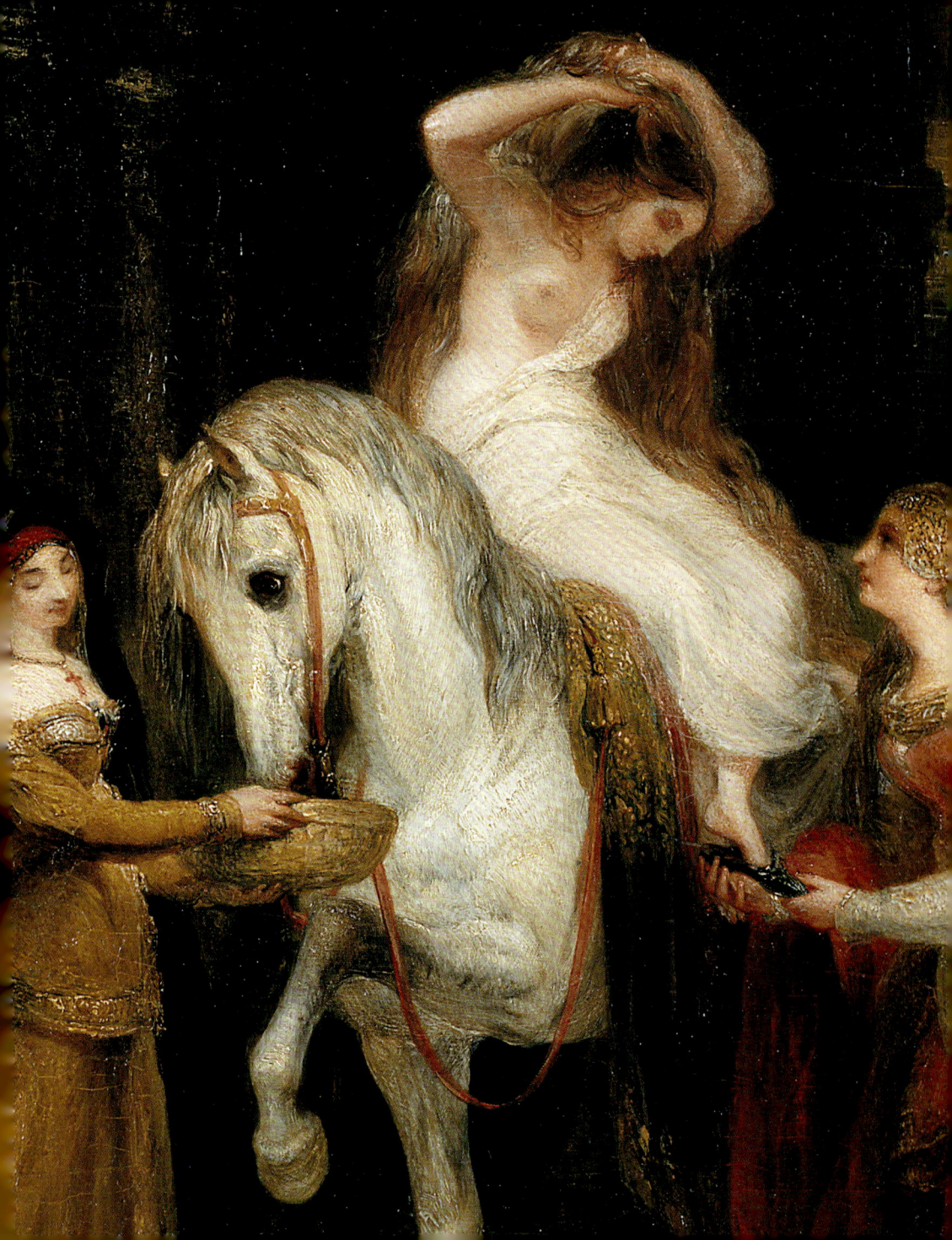

Horses in their splendour and strength have attained a supernatural and mystical status in the imagination of world-wide civilisations. Mythological horses inspire heroism, serve as companions, represent our worst impulses and connect humans to higher powers and ancient civilisations. Artists visualise the mythical horse to create imagery that is not confined by reality but has a more imaginative and liberated nature; metaphorically unbridled and wild. These fictional horses often serve artists' own ideologies and beliefs, or manifest their fantasies. The mythical horse in art stirs a sense of grandeur by placing humans and their noble steeds at vital moments in history and legends, each loaded with symbolic imagery. The lores of early Britain evoke mystery and gallantry, which artists translate into sculpture and paintings, or craft their compositions to convey the wonder and majesty of bold tales. This imagery creatively challenges the world and our relationship to horses within it. Captured by the hand of artists, wild or otherworldly horses become tameable whilst simultaneously set free to charge through our imaginations.

George Jones, *Godiva Preparing to Ride through Coventry* exhibited 1833 (detail, see p.71)

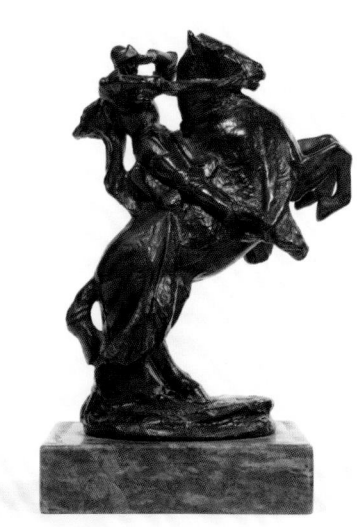

William Reid Dick 1878–1961
St George and the Dragon (for E.V. Lucas) 1914
Bronze on stone base 16.2 × 8.9 × 10.8

In a version of the legend of the venerated soldier St George,
he slays a dragon while on horseback. Horrified by his discovery
that the inhabitants of a village have been satiating this dragon
with livestock and eventually human tributes, the brave St George
offers to fight the dragon, and wins. Dick's sculpture captures
the rousing moment when St George sits astride a wide-eyed
horse rearing in attack. His left hand firmly grips the reins while
he shields his eyes with his right, perhaps to aid him spot
the dragon. St George's billowing cape and the strong diagonal
created by the horse's body gives the sculpture a sense of
unwavering movement as, undeterred, the hero presses forward.

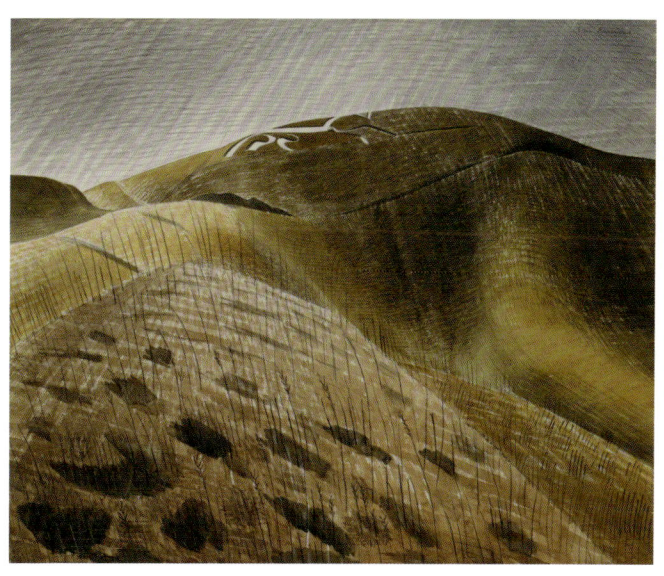

Eric Ravilious 1903–42
The Vale of the White Horse c.1939
Graphite and watercolour on paper 45.1 × 32.4

Amid a landscape of gently undulating hills, White Horse Hill
is visible in the distance. It is part of a site of complex ancient
remains where St George is said to have slain the dragon while
riding his white horse. The area's Bronze Age inhabitants filled
deep trenches with white chalk to outline the 110m image
of the prehistoric horse after which the hill is now named, and
Ravilious's watercolour shows its geometric torso, tail and limbs.
There is no other sign of human intervention in this rainy
landscape apart from the horse, suggesting secrets hidden just
beyond our understanding. Despite the horse's distance from
the foreground of the picture, Ravilious's low viewpoint and the
preceding hills signify the magnitude of the white horse.

William Blake 1757–1827
God Judging Adam 1795
Relief etching, ink and watercolour on paper 43.2 × 53.5

Two horses with flames for tails and manes pull a fiery chariot,
curling their heads in so deeply that their noses are close
to their chests. The graceful arch of the neck, at first, appears
beautiful. To create this pose, however, the horses hold
themselves with tension – a contraction that creates an
imbalance counterproductive to efficient movement. The
horses' posture echo the attributes of Urizen, the godlike
figure in the chariot. In Blake's own mythology, Urizen's laws
limit human imagination. Here he condemns a naked and
elderly Adam for tasting the forbidden fruit. Although Blake
was a committed Christian, he was hostile to many forms of
organised religion including the Church of England.

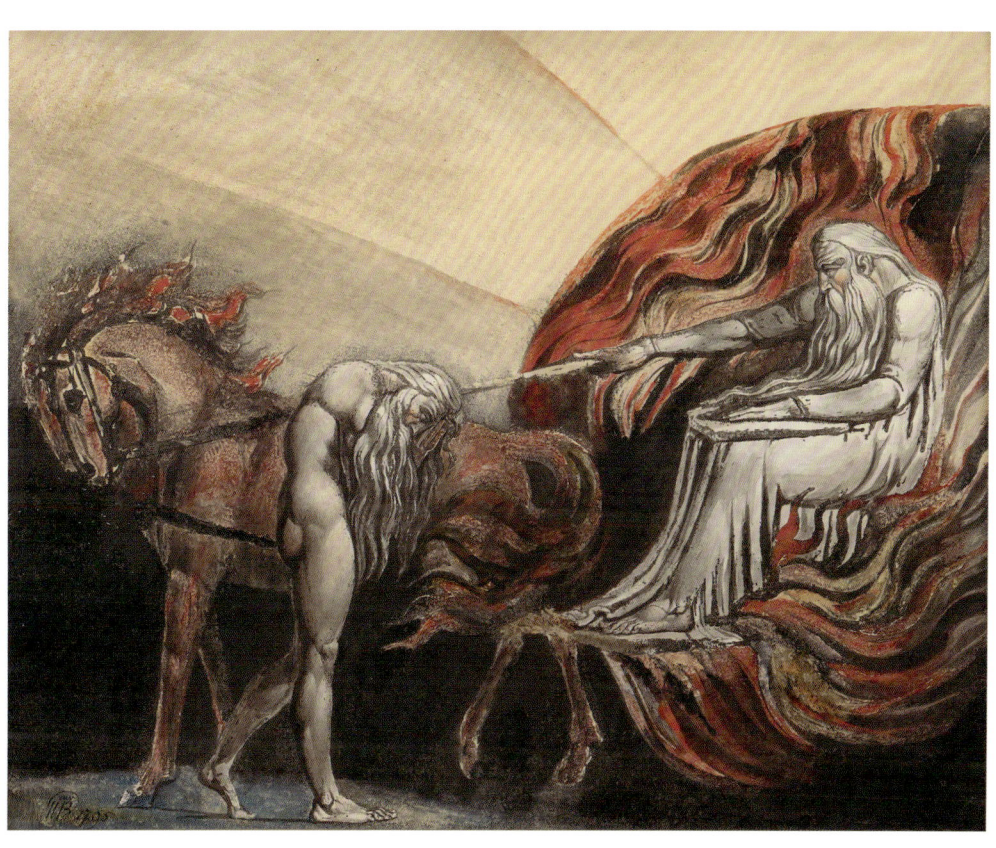

Christopher Le Brun born 1951
Dream, Think, Speak 1981–2
Oil paint on canvas 244 × 228.5

Horses are a common feature in Le Brun's work, alongside trees, forests, towers and wandering figures. In *Dream, Think, Speak*, a white horse occupies the centre of the composition, accompanied by the head of a second ghost-like horse on the right. The black forms that tower behind them are evocative of wings, although the artist does not describe his horse as winged and they may rather be trees. The landscape is dark, dreamlike and ominous. Le Brun does not draw his images from life or source material, but invents them or remakes them from memory. His brushwork is expressive, and the physical trace of the bold and textured brushstrokes on the canvas here echoes the idea of translating dreams into what can be experienced by others.

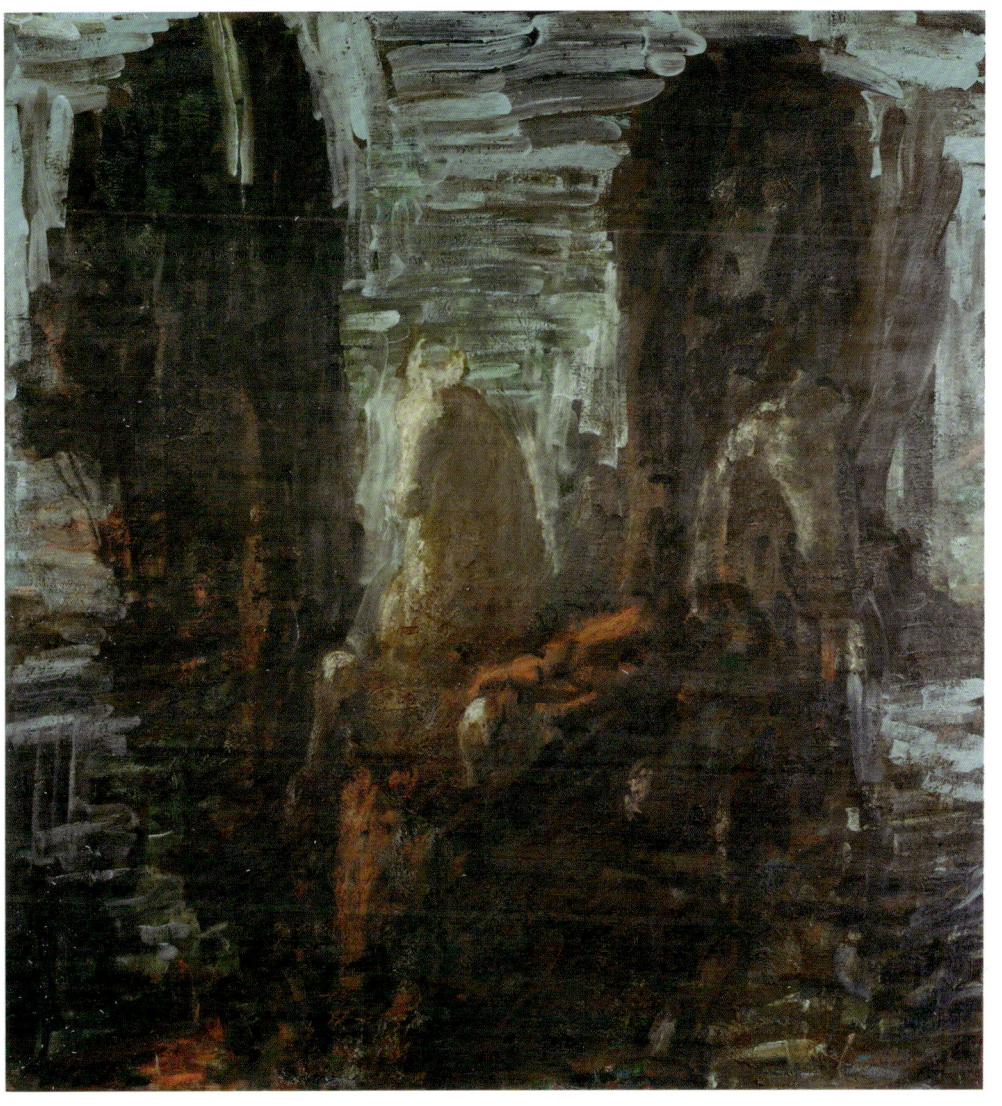

George Jones 1768–1869
Godiva Preparing to Ride through Coventry exhibited 1833
Oil paint on mahogany 74.9 × 61

According to legend, the eleventh-century gentlewoman
Lady Godiva is known for a legendary ride through Coventry
in Warwickshire, naked. She had been moved by the plight of
Coventry's residents caused by her husband's tyrannical taxes,
and pleaded with him on the townsfolk's behalf. He agreed to
lower these taxes on one condition, which he hoped his demure
wife would refuse: that she ride through Coventry without any
clothes on. Jones paints her as she undresses and prepares
to ride through the streets, covered only by the long hair she
coiffes. The artist includes many references to his subject's
piety: the adoring gazes of her companions, a prominent red
cross on the chest of the woman furthest left, and the white
horse. Its coat and Lady Godiva's robe and pale skin form the
brightest part of the dark composition. The horse affirms Lady
Godiva's high moral standing, piety, purity and compassion.

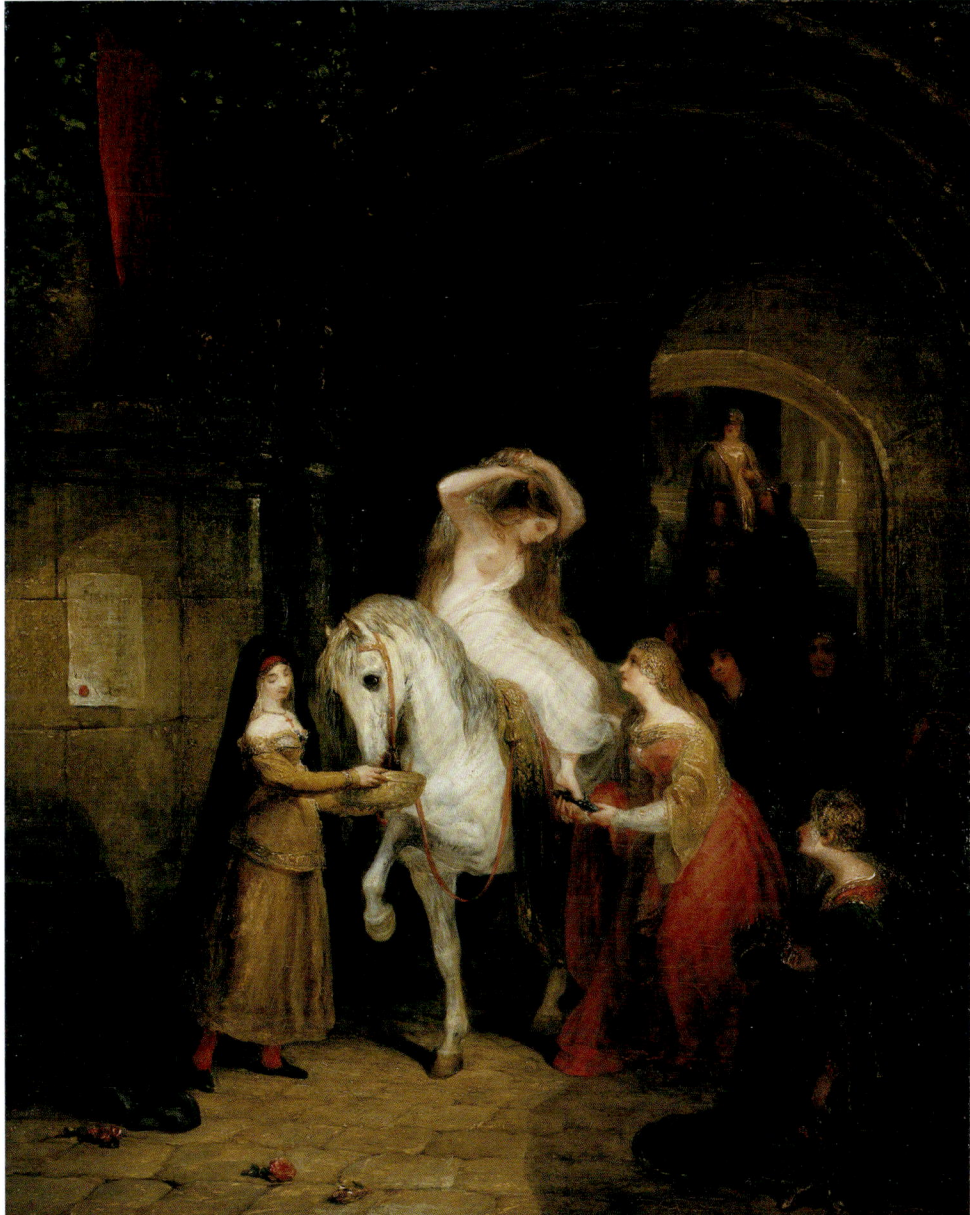

Mark Wallinger born 1959
Ghost 2001
Scanachrome print on aluminium lightbox 295 × 249 × 18

Standing almost three metres high, this imposing aluminium
lightbox illuminates a digital photograph of a horse with a spiralled
horn. The horse is Whistlejacket, the famous racehorse painted
by George Stubbs around 1762 (see p.22). Mark Wallinger, who
frequently references well known British artworks, photographed
Stubbs's oil painting and added a horn based on the tusk of a
narwal to the image. As in Stubbs's picture, there are no people
in Wallinger's image, nor a landscape; all attention is on the
mighty and mythical creature, which appears spectral, echoing
the title of the work. Like a ghost, too, the monumentality,
drama and expressiveness of Stubbs's painting lingers in
Wallinger's work. This contemporary version of *Whistlejacket*
continues to evoke British horse-racing traditions.

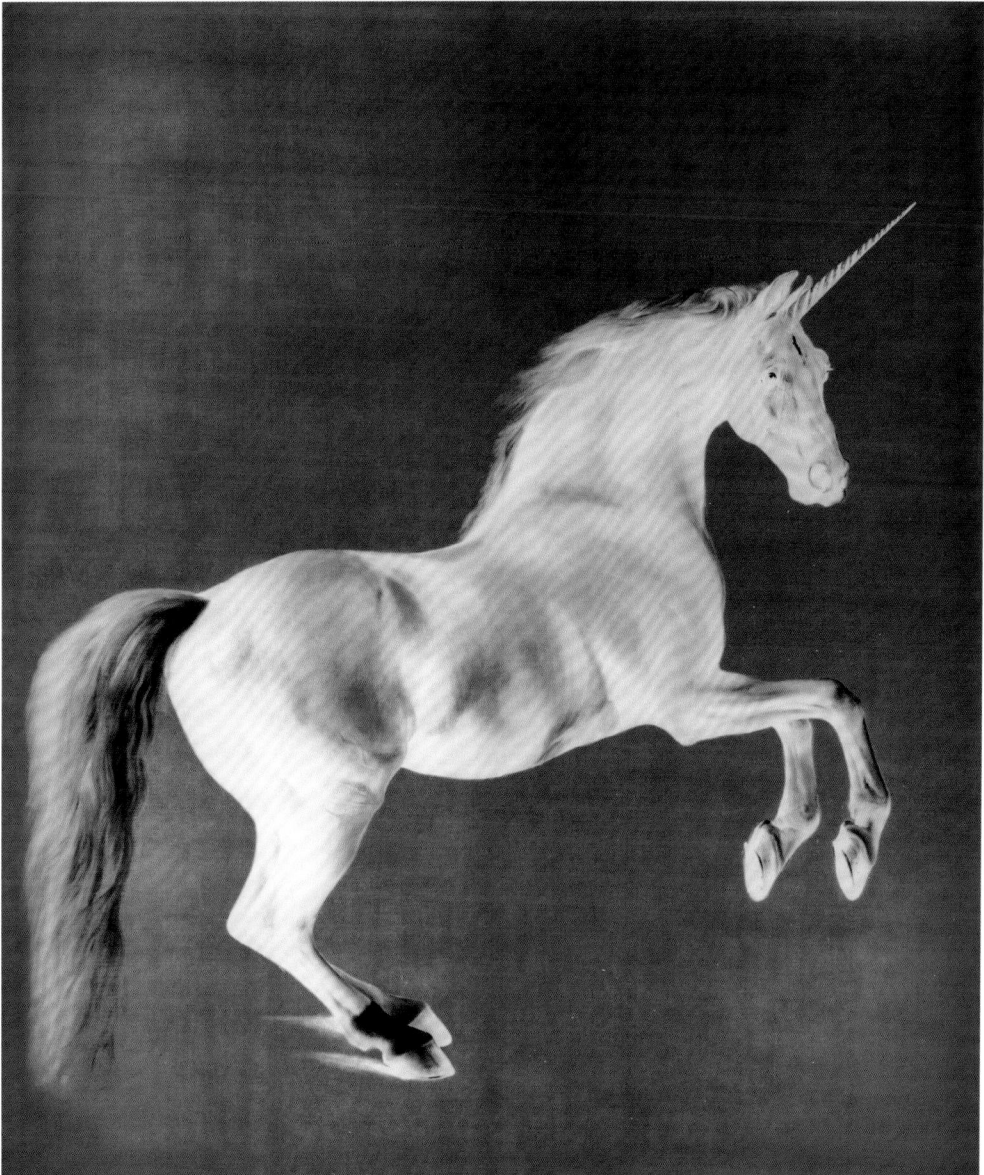

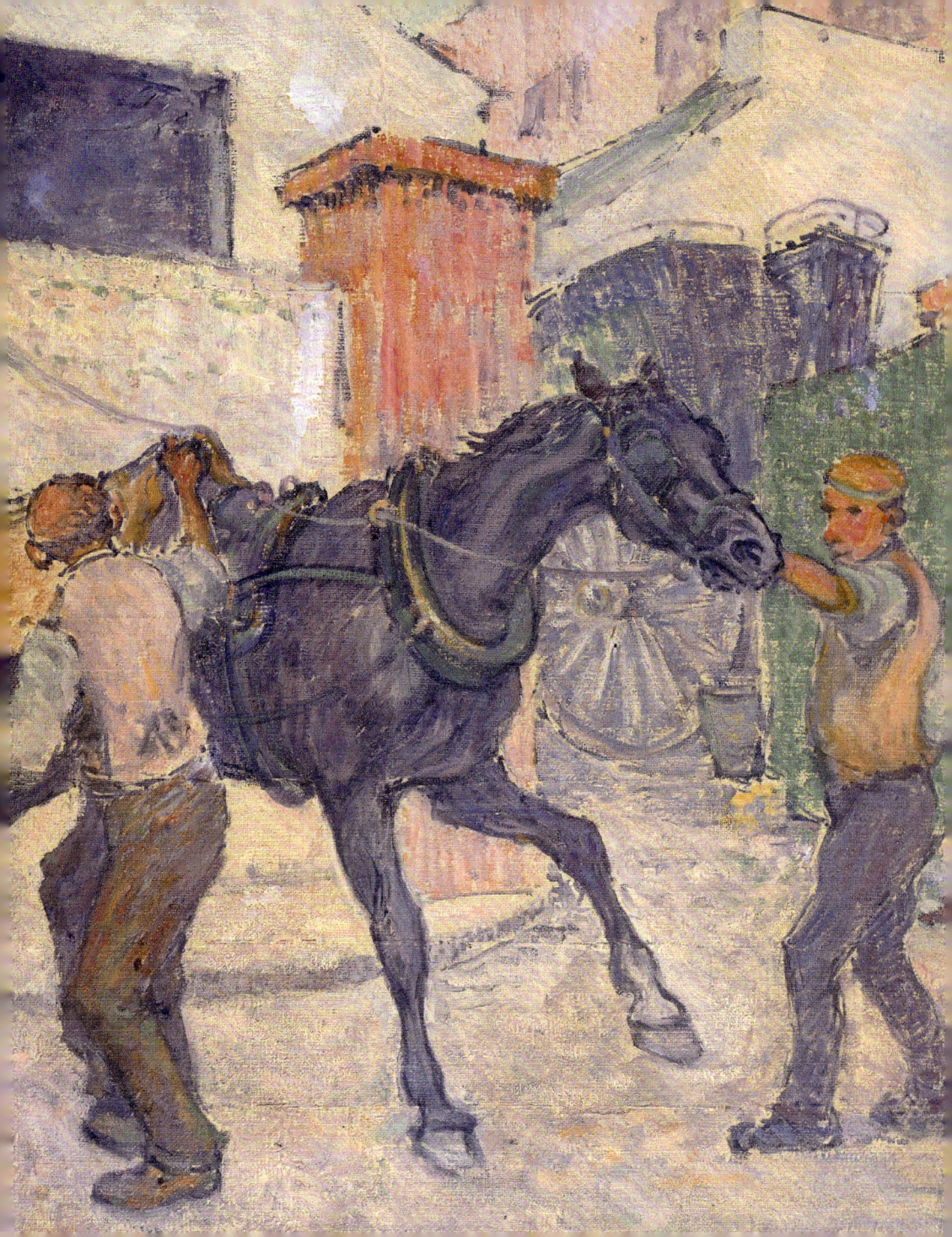

Transportation

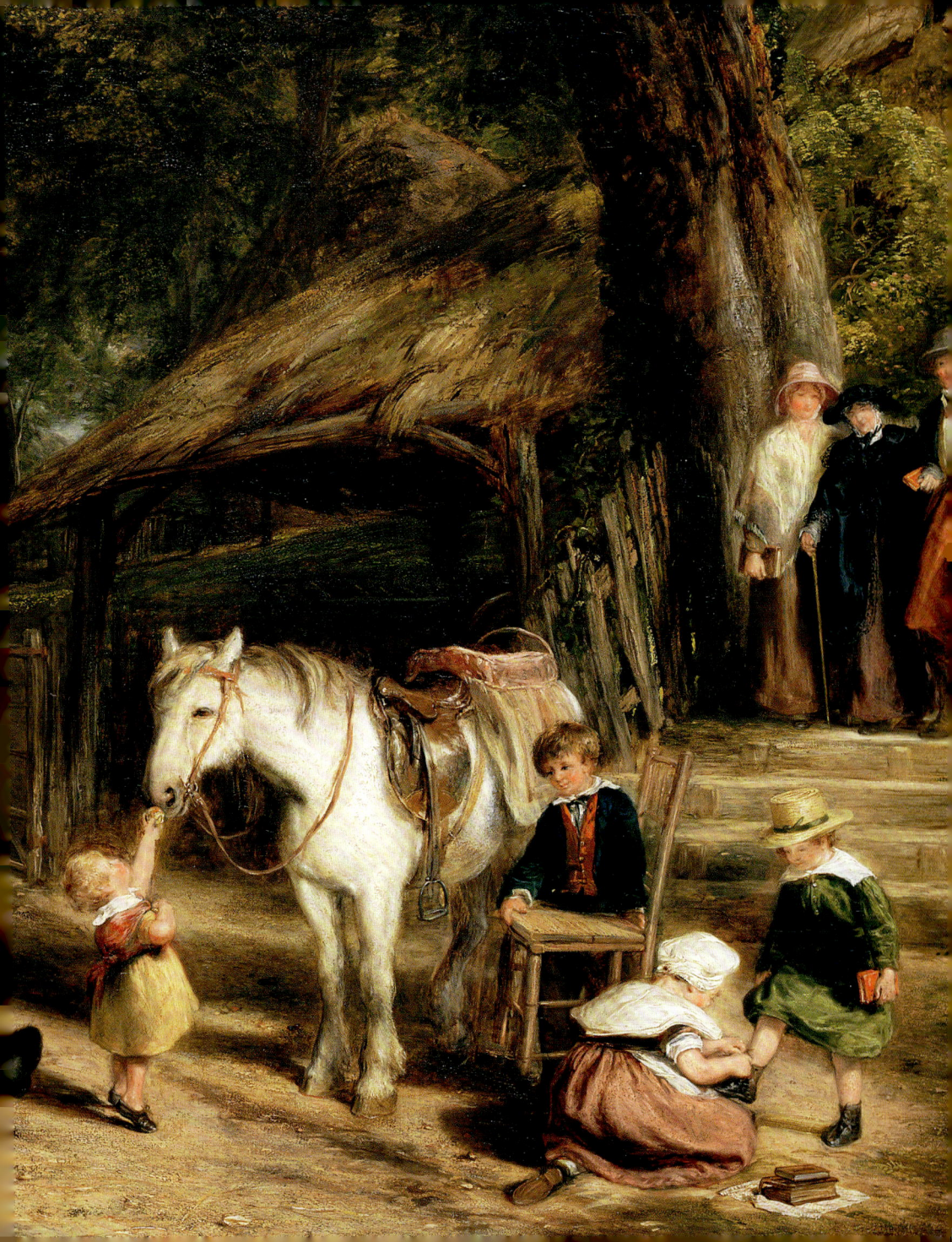

Horses run fast and far, making them ideal for the transportation of passengers and goods. Artists have depicted horses delivering armies into battle and transporting otherworldly figures across mythological realms. They have also portrayed horses on more mundane journeys such as transporting rural labourers across fields, carrying the elderly to church and drawing the carriages of holidaymakers in foreign locations. While men dominate the imagery of horses at work, in conflict and on the racetrack, women and children are more present in the visualisation of horses in transportation. The working class, making deliveries or driving cabs, also emerge in these images. Depictions of the everyday movement of people and goods signify societal shifts in Britain between the eighteenth and twentieth centuries. Horse-drawn transport enabled work opportunities further from home, leading to a decrease in regional divisions as people travelled to other cities and towns for entertainment and leisure with less difficulty. The decline of the representation of the horse in transport marks a further societal shift, the introduction of motor transport and the railways. The horse as a symbol of speed, distance and connection became less potent than that of the locomotive, as cars and trains ran faster and farther.

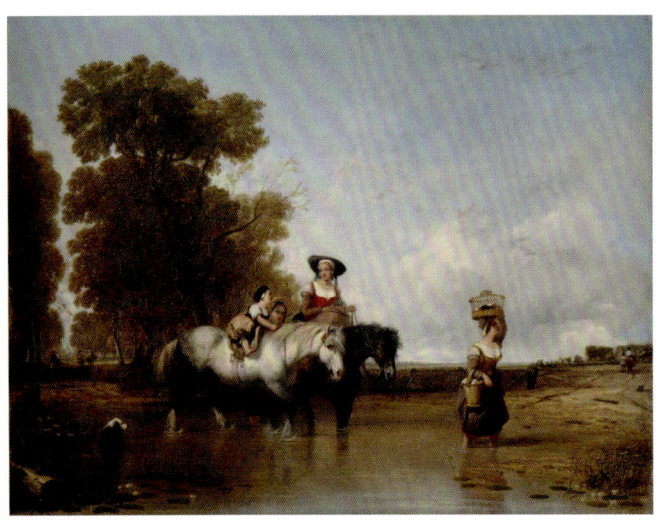

Augustus Wall Callcott 1779–1844
Returning from Market exhibited 1834
Oil paint on canvas 109.2 × 144.8

Depictions of women riding horses, especially so casually, are
rare in British art. In the early nineteenth century, women horse
riders were of the genteel or upper classes, riding for leisure, or
women from the labouring class who rode on family farms to or
from the fields. The two small riding horses in Callcott's painting
walk gently through a stream. Their relaxed gait, and the fact
that they have been trusted with the toddler, suggests that
these horses are dependable and of a gentle nature. Horses are
central to this rural scene: still more populate the path on
either side of this group.

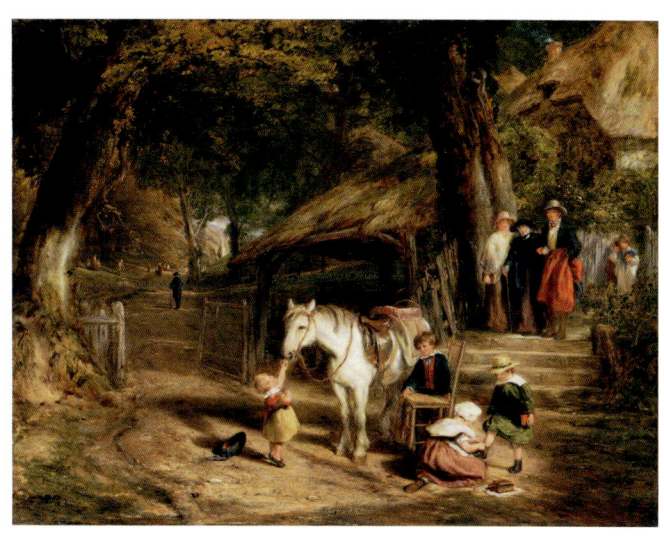

William Collins 1788–1847
Sunday Morning possibly exhibited 1836
Oil paint on canvas 81.3 × 106.7

Collins's nostalgic scene shows a middle-class family preparing
to go to church. A dappled grey pony is in the middle of the
composition, between the elderly grandmother descending the
steps and the church visible through the trees in the distance.
The animal waits patiently to carry its frail rider as a young
boy approaches it with a chair to assist her into the saddle. By
riding, the grandmother can join the throng of country folk on
the distant path and partake in the Sunday service. The humble
pony appears intelligent and friendly, unperturbed by the
children's activity around it as it sniffs the apple proffered to it.
Collins's soft, earthy palette creates a calm atmosphere where
the pony is in harmony with the humans.

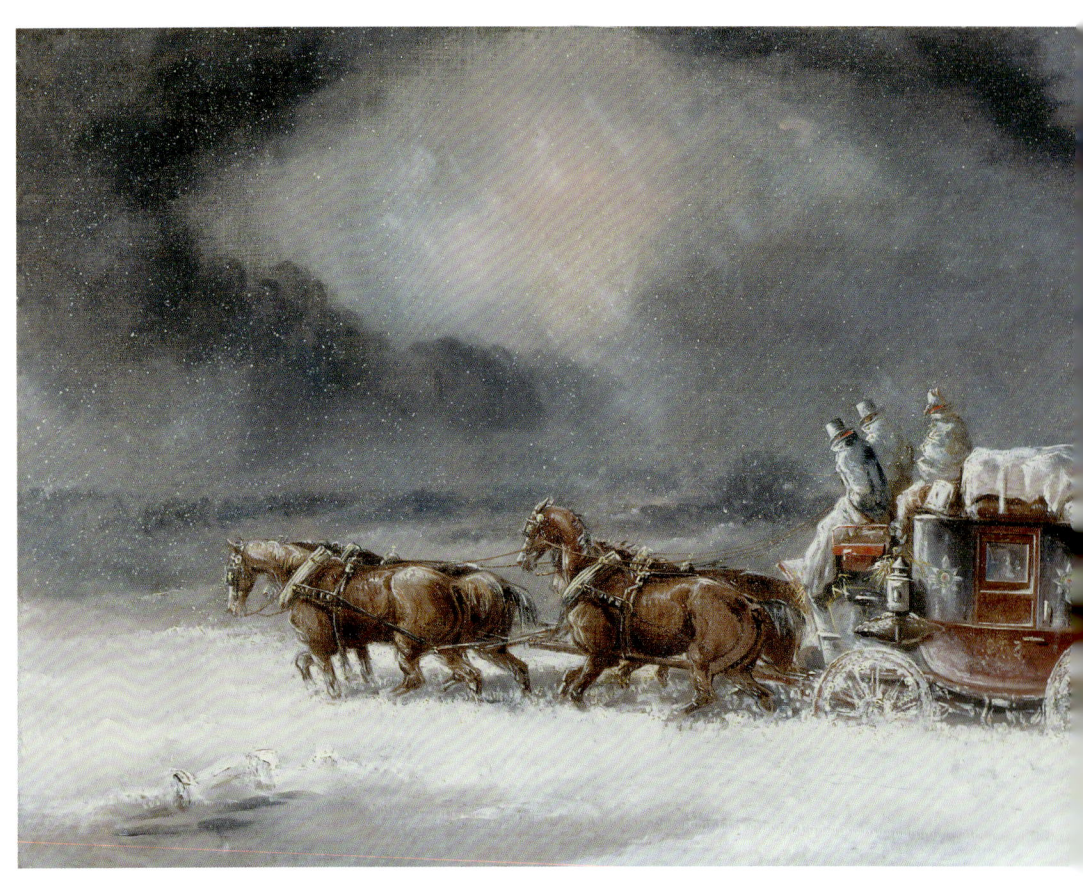

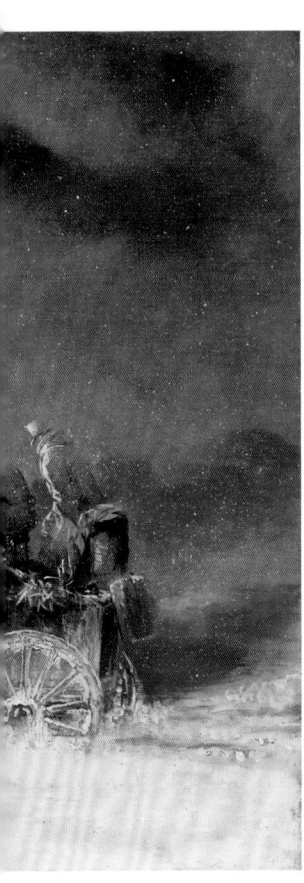

Charles Cooper Henderson 1803–77
Mail Coach in a Snowstorm c.1835–40
Oil paint on canvas 45.4 × 76.5

A Royal Mail coach carries post from London, or to the capital
with post from other towns and cities. We cannot tell which:
the lettering on the carriage door indicating the destination is
fully obscured by the snow, while the company crest below is
barely visible. Henderson's horses strain forward on what looks
like an impassable road, which in the early nineteenth century
would have probably been no more than a well-worn mud track.
Other horses would be stationed at roughly ten-mile intervals
along the route, poised to relieve these. At the time of the
painting, Royal Mail coaches pulled by horses were some of the
fastest vehicles to cross long distances and stopped only for
postal business. The demise of horse-drawn mail carriages
began in 1830 with the first transportation of mail on the railways.

John Frederick Lewis 1805–76
Spanish Couple Riding a Mule c.1832–4
Chalk and gouache on paper 27.3 × 35.6

Lewis's mule takes up the centre of the composition. Its
stillness – and the slightly dejected countenance of the man and
woman – hint at a long journey behind or still to come. The man
sits astride the mule, facing forward, while the woman sits
side-saddle. Perhaps her skirts are heavy, or she is protecting
her modesty by riding this way, as was encouraged for women
riders in several cultures across time. Lewis shows his skill in
rendering different textures in muted colours: both the mule
and the woman wear layers of textured garments and fabrics,
some richly decorated. The chalk and gouache simultaneously
show the coarseness of the mule's coat and the smoothness
of the pink top that covers the woman's legs.

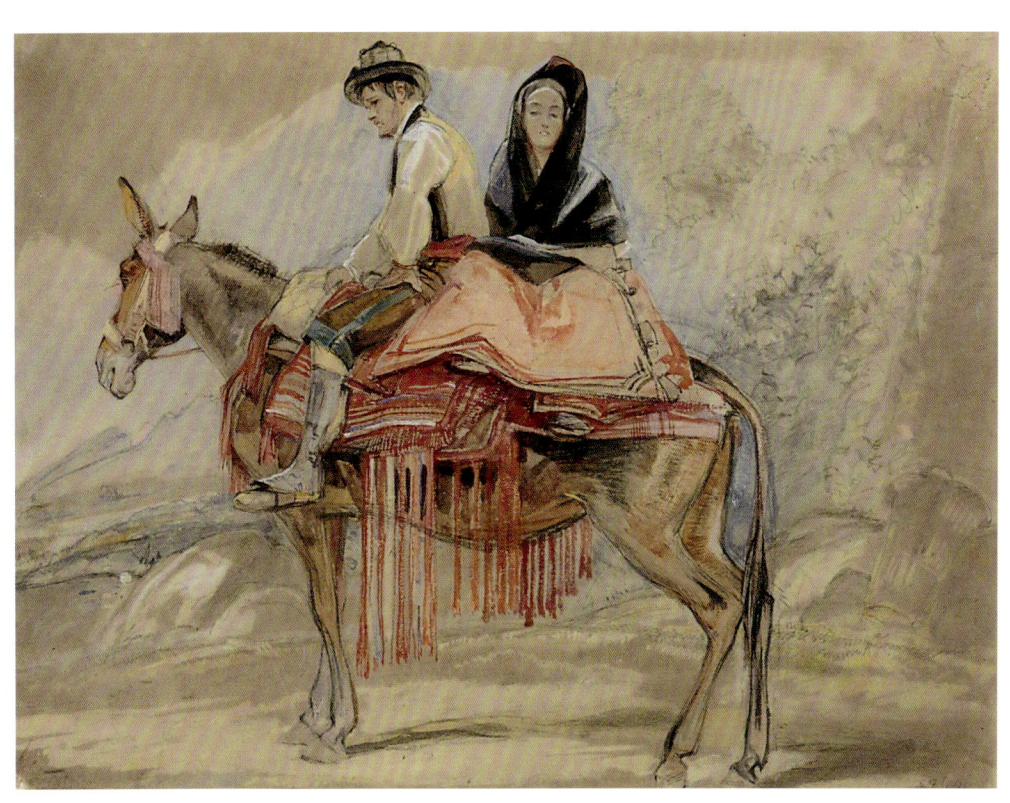

Robert Bevan 1865–1925
The Cab Horse c.1910
Oil paint on canvas 63.5 × 76.2

The Cab Horse was painted at a time when traditional horse-drawn cabs were being replaced by motor cars. Here, two men release a horse from the shafts of the two-wheeled carriage known as a hansom cab. The scene bristles with movement: the man on the left throws a blanket over the horse's hindquarters, signalling the end of its workday, while the smiling, ruddy-complexioned man on the right attempts to manoeuvre the horse into position, resulting in the animal staggering back awkwardly. Espousing the Camden Art Group's ethos of painting moments of everyday city life, Bevan sought out scenes of the urban working horse. His use of colour is anti-realist and adventurous; the horse is in complementary hues of violet and purple. This liberation from realistic depiction gives the painting a modern feel.

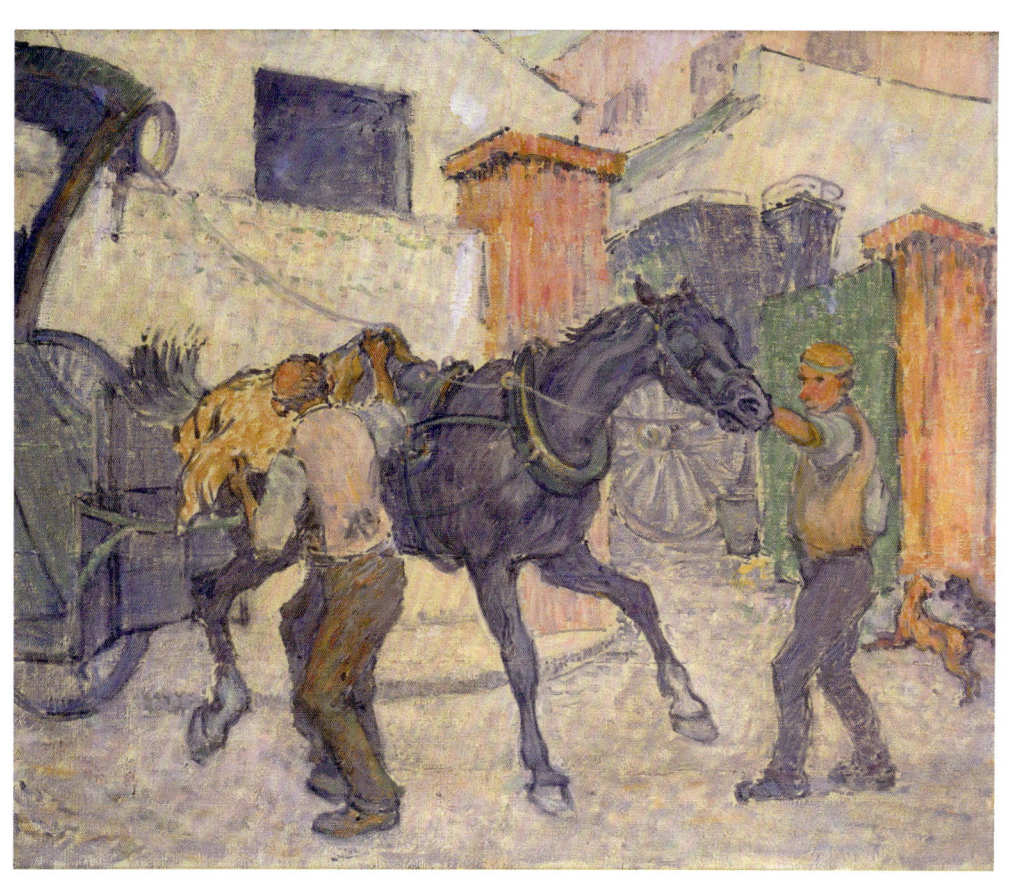

Tom Gentleman 1882–1966
Grey Horses 1946
Lithograph on paper 49.6 × 76.5

In the centre of a bustling village street are two white horses
and a round-topped wagon labelled 'McMullens Ales' on the
side. The man in the wagon is unloading a crate of ale while
another rolls a barrel towards one of the buildings. A boy in blue
– the artist's son – is seen admiring the drays, horses adapted
for carrying heavy loads. Gentleman's stylised image was
produced as part of School Prints, a scheme created in the
spirit of post-war optimism to increase children's access to
contemporary art. The colours are bright and within a limited
and harmonious palette range, while the forms of the buildings,
people and horses are simple. There is a sense of joy in the
gentle productivity of the horses and villagers.

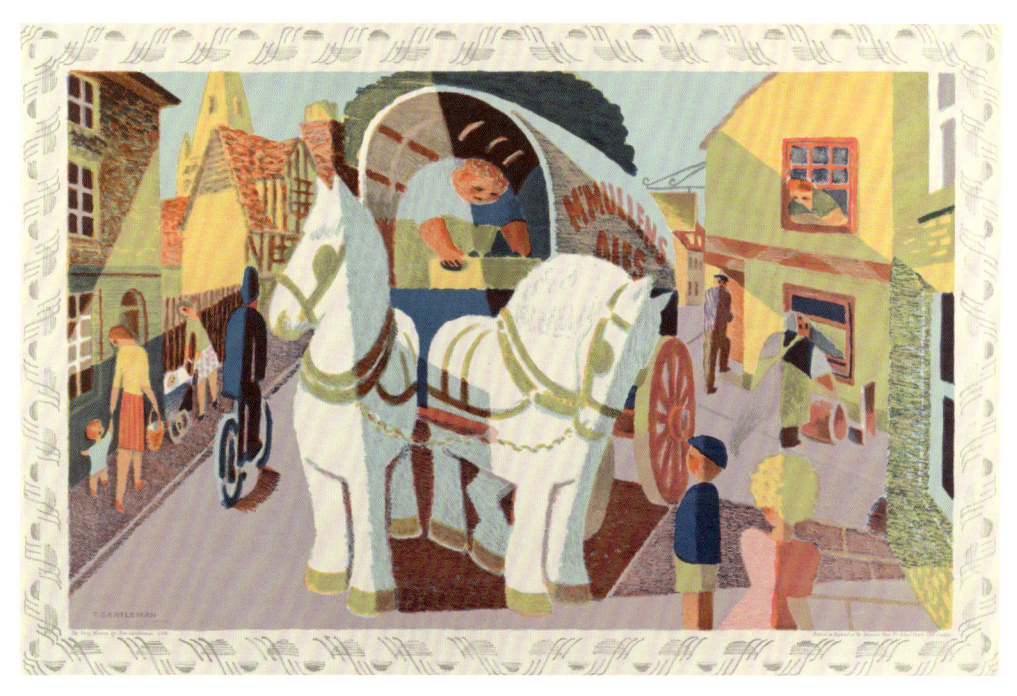

Eileen Agar 1899–1991
Photograph of a horse and carriage 1949
Negative photograph 6.2 × 6.1

A horse pauses at the side of the road in Sorrento, Italy.
Perhaps it is a local breed. It is pulling a type of phaeton, a light,
sporty, owner-driven open carriage. To judge from the state of
its legs, the horse is likely in pain: its hooves are overgrown with
contracted, or shrunken, heels, and its hocks – the equivalent of
a human ankle – are turned inwards, a precursor to permanent
lameness. The horse is unable to deliver its weight evenly or
absorb shock properly. Its compromised health is at odds with
the nature of this photo, which Agar took on one of her trips
with her husband. The subjects of her photo albums are largely
joyous and include landscapes, seaside towns and villages and
group photographs with friends. Although it is likely and
understandable that Agar would not have known as much, this
horse suffered to facilitate her travel and leisure.

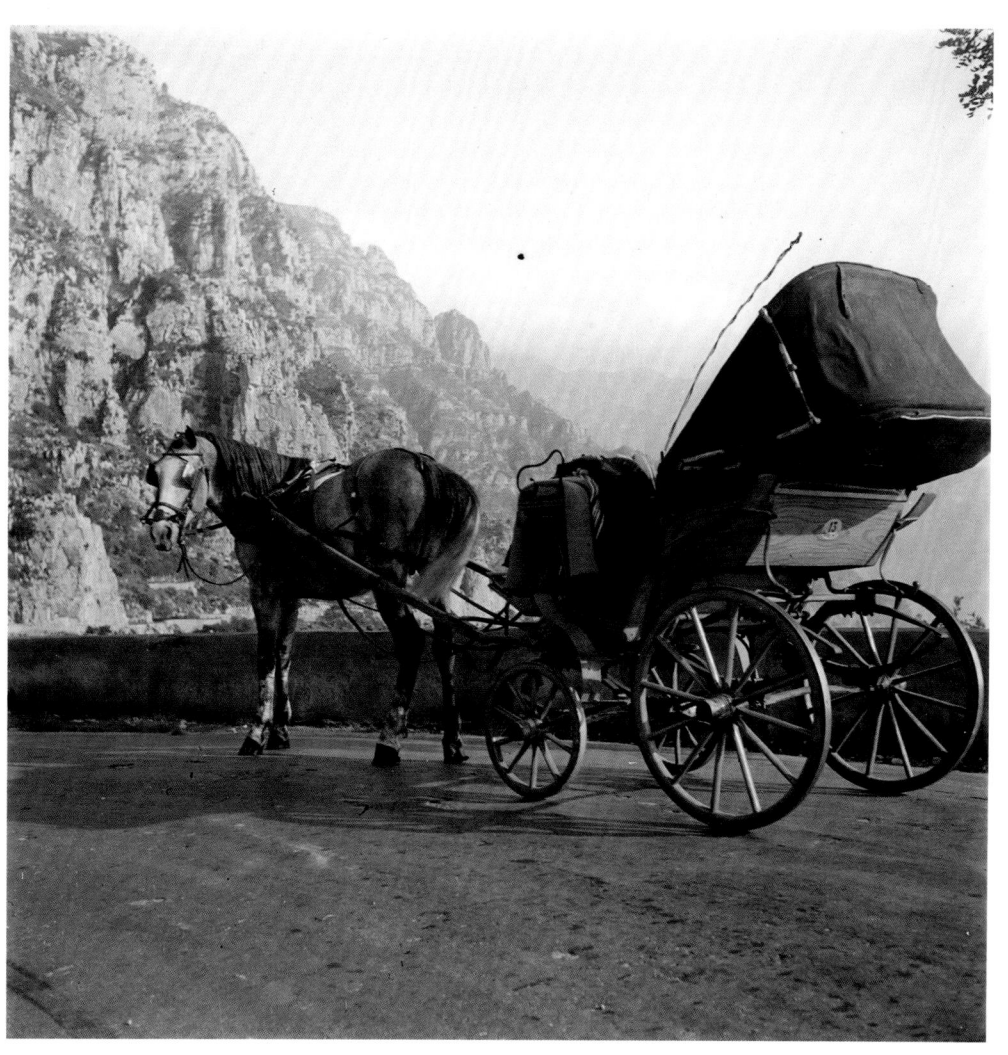

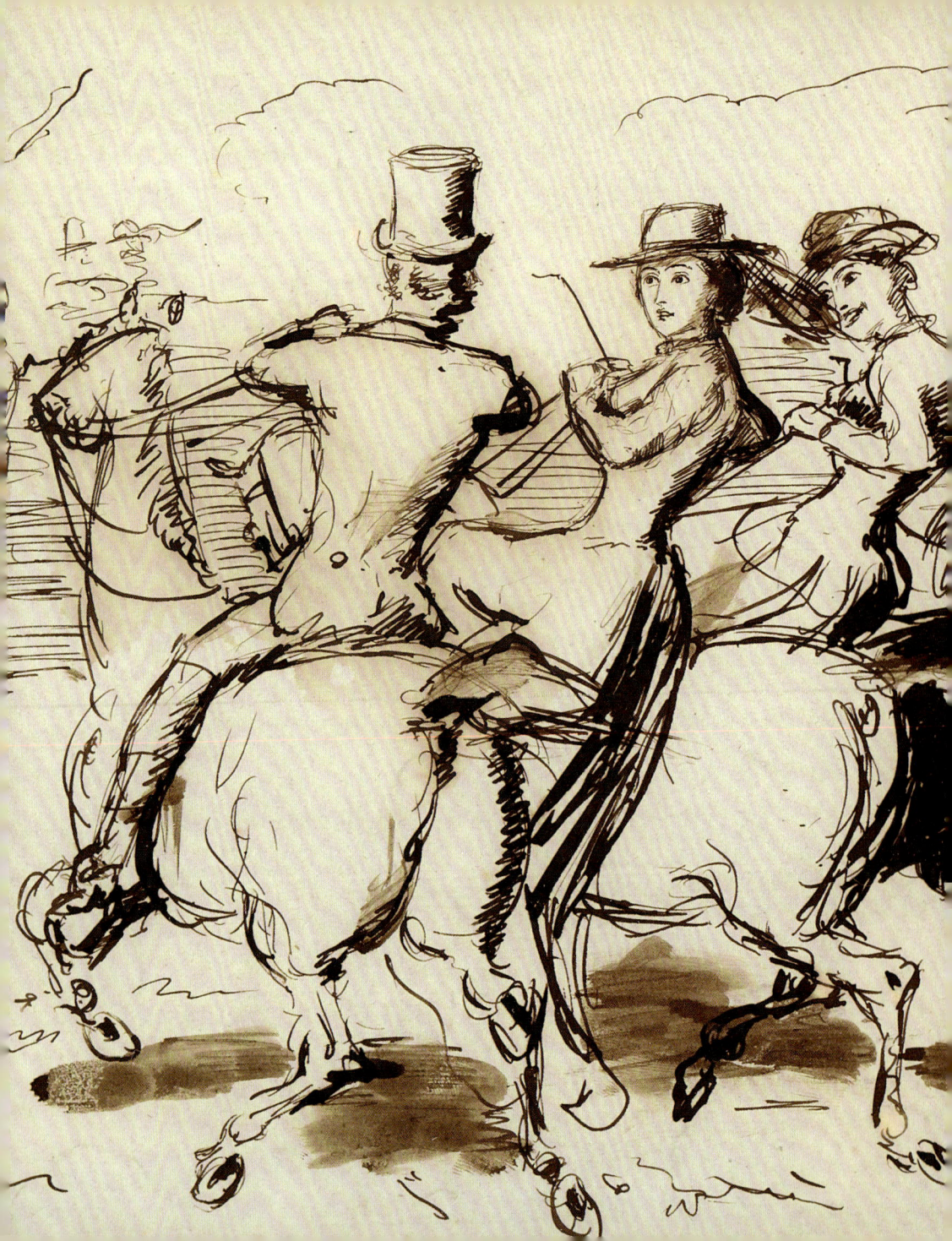

Leisure

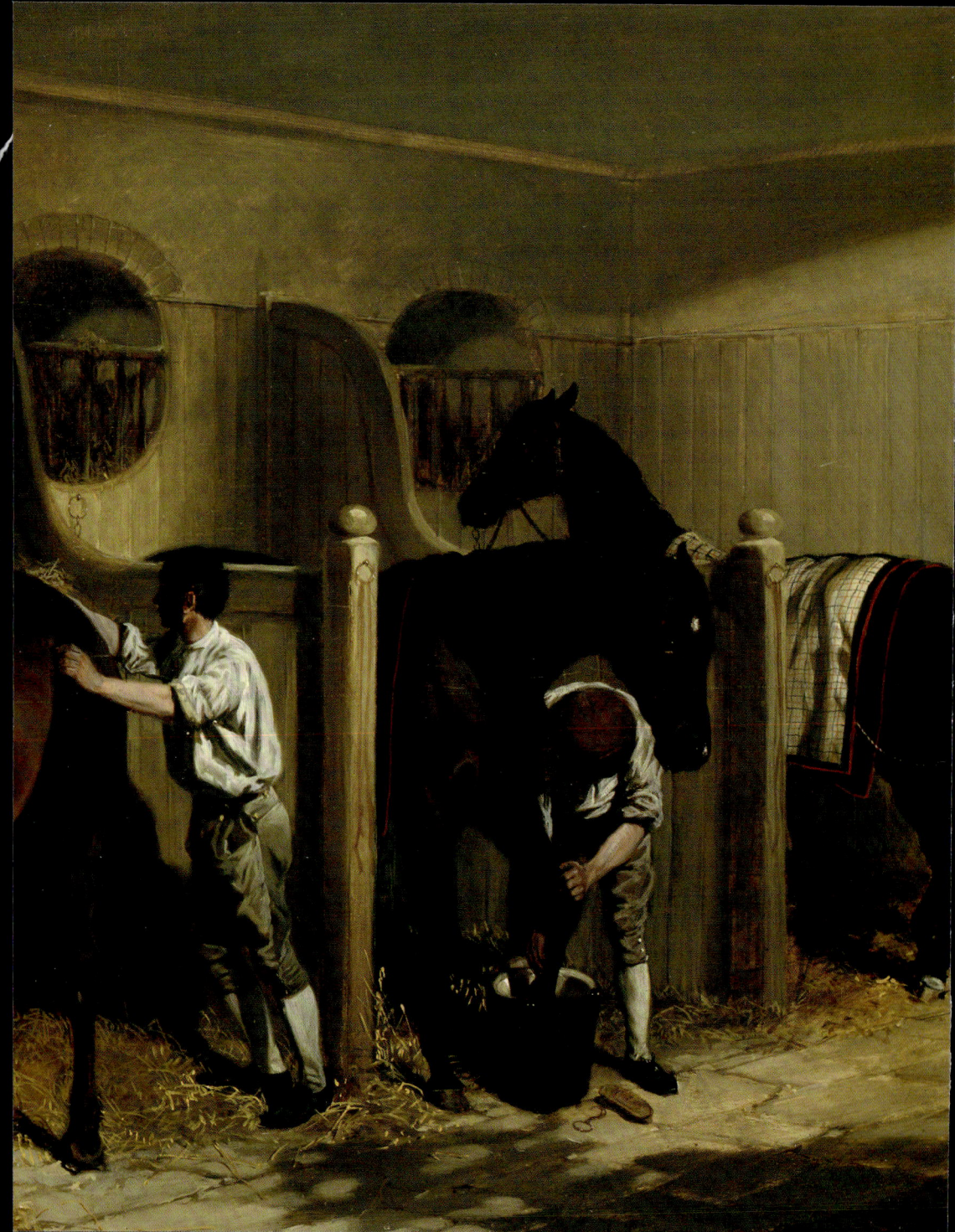

In scenes of leisure, horses are associated with jubilation and pleasure. A sense of thrill and liberty arises from the vision of a horse speeding forward on an open plain. A powerful and athletic hunter, seen at rest, can stir in the imagination expectations of an exhilarating chase without depicting the gore of the kill. The spectacle of horse choreography executed gracefully delights. Artists have captured the expressive collaboration between horse and rider as teammates connected in the rhythmic gallop of a hunt, sudden turn on a sports field or leap during a performance. At times, the horse serves to highlight the sportsman's prowess in controlling an imposing creature. As with the image of the horse in transportation, artists documented societal shifts under this theme of leisure. By the nineteenth century, horse riding purely for pleasure in the countryside and through city parks had become popular for the middle classes, their steeds symbolising the rider's sophistication and refinement. Where the working class appear in this visual culture, they are included as labourers. Social order, spectacle and sport combine in the image of the horse in leisure.

Charles Cooper Henderson 1803–77
Sportsmen in Scottish Dress Driving to the Moors c.1845
Oil paint on canvas 33 × 61.3

A bay with a docked tail pulls a two-wheeled cart, assisted by
a smaller pony hitched alongside it. The shafts on the cart are
designed to fit on either side of a single horse, suggesting that
the cargo is heavier than intended for this type of vehicle. Four
sportsmen are crowded into the small cart. They are dressed
similarly in plaids and traditional Scottish hats and bonnets. The
men are surrounded by their hunting guns, game bags, a red
flask, hamper and retriever, and appear happy as they speed
through the Scottish hills. Their way of travel during their day
of shooting is simple and efficient.

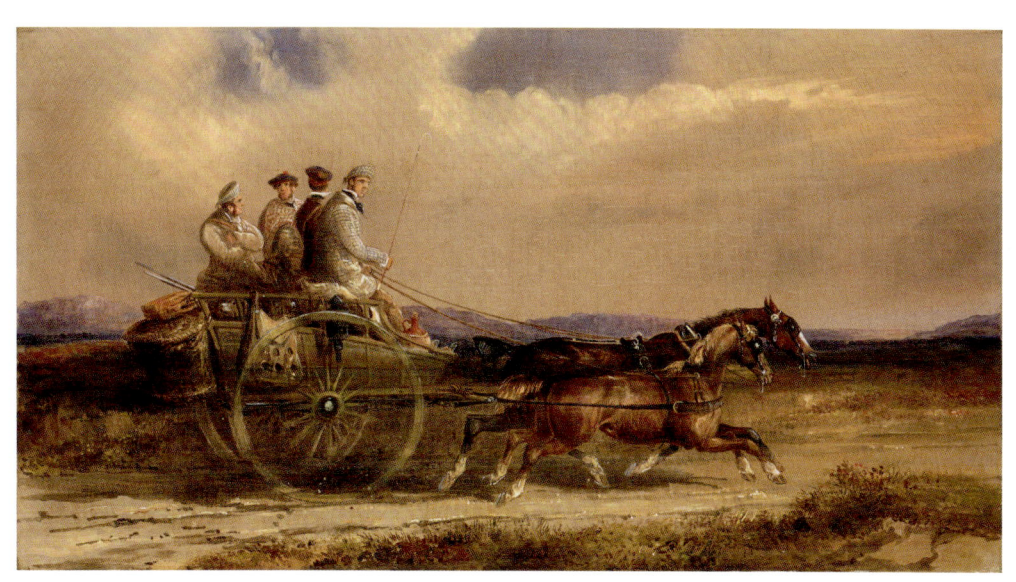

John Wootton c.1682–1764
*Viscount Weymouth's Hunt: The Hon. John Spencer
beside a Hunter held by a Young Boy* 1733–6
Oil paint on canvas 345 × 256

John Spencer and his athletic hunter stand in a lush landscape,
both of them gazing directly at the viewer. They are part of
a hunt. The horse raises its head and hind leg, swishing its tail.
It is attentive to its rider, the groom, dogs and its surroundings,
perhaps excited or uneasy. Wootton's depiction may not be an
accurate depiction of the breed, but his artistic interpretation
of it. The horse appears to have a white patch (known as a snip)
on its nose and a white star on its forehead, and its foot markings
are attentively painted: a white sock on its right foreleg, a shorter
pastern above the hoof on its left fore, and on its hind legs what
look like half-pasterns or coronets. This is the first in a set of
paintings of *Viscount Weymouth's Hunt* made by Wootton.

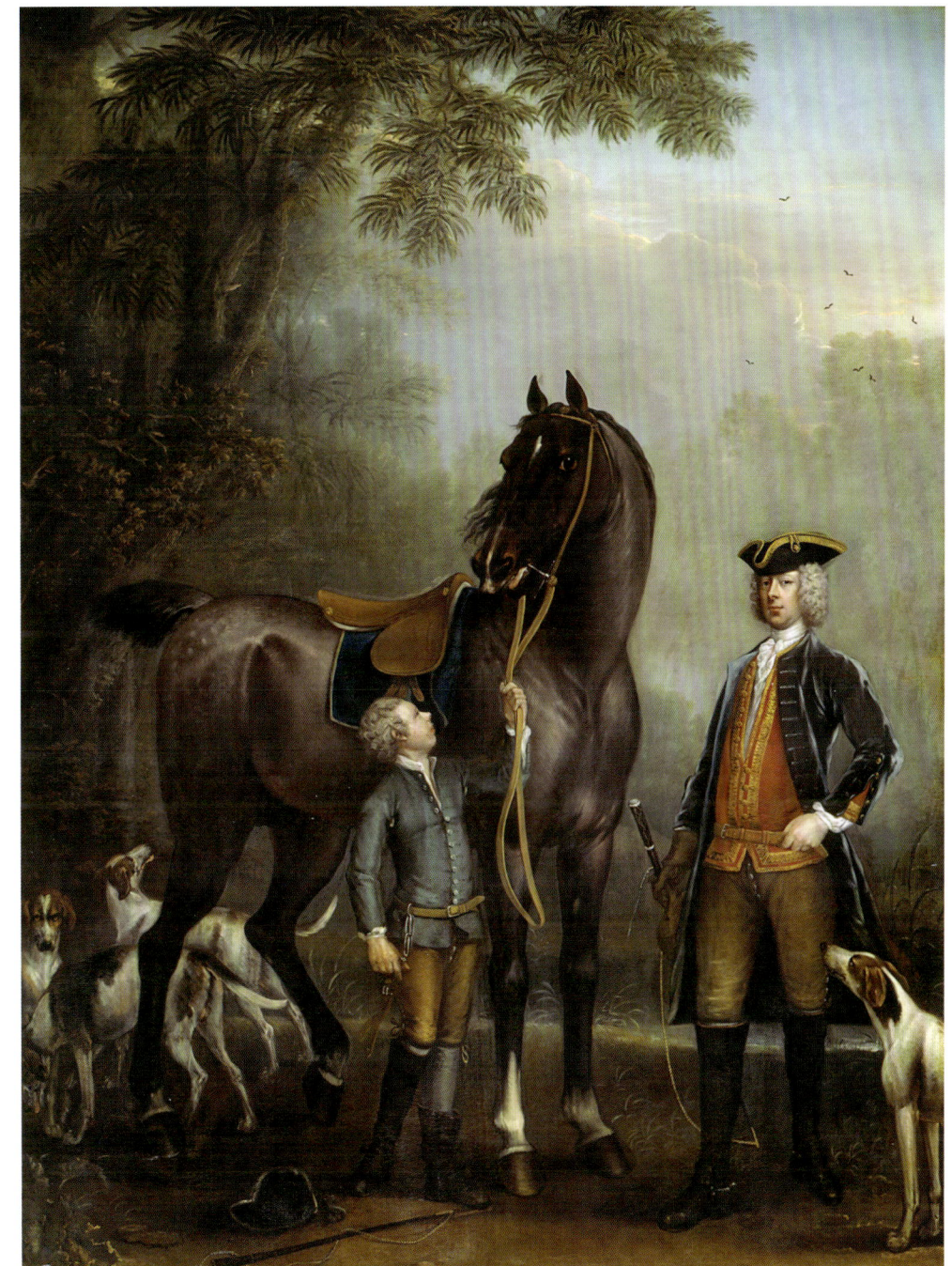

John Frederick Herring 1795–1865
The Hunting Stud 1845
Oil paint on canvas 45.4 × 70.8

Self-taught artist Herring captures the anatomy and
temperament of four hunting studs. Although they are at
almost opposite ends of the colour spectrum, the two horses
on the left have coats that are equally vibrant. The horses are
tethered to their stalls yet exude a vivid sense of movement.
The grey or white horse closest to us looks back frightfully,
bending and contracting one hind leg at the stifle joint (the
equivalent of the human knee), perhaps in response to having
his sheath cleaned by the groom. A second groom is rubbing
down the next horse along, perhaps to remove sweat after a hunt,
while the third horse is having its feet soaked to remove dirt
and prevent sores. These horses are meticulously cared for.

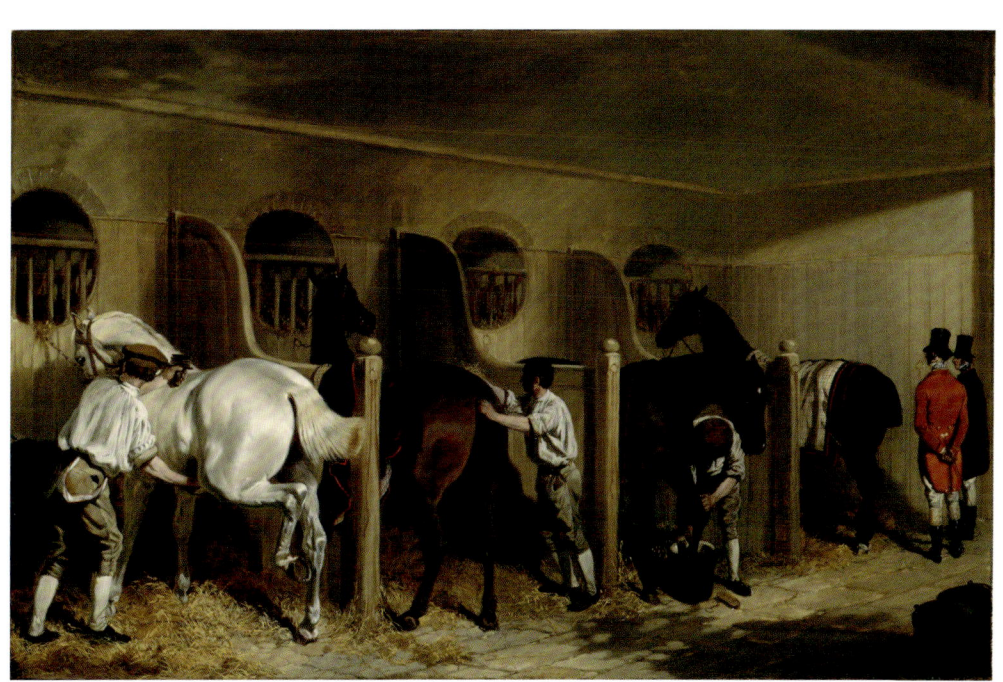

Rose English born 1950
Quadrille 1975, 2013
21 photographs, gelatin silver prints on paper; 2 photographs,
c-prints on paper; ink on paper; horse hooves; horse hair;
synthetic horse hair; textiles; leather; wood; metal; film, super
8mm, shown as video, colour

These photographs are part of the documentation of a
performance that took place at the 1975 Southampton Horse
Show. Six dancers in costumes which included high horse
hooves and tails performed a quadrille, a carefully
choreographed horse ride commonly accompanied by music.
The audience was taken by surprise; the intervention was a
departure from the standard equestrian programming. English,
part of a generation of women artists in the 1970s whose
performance art sought to challenge social, gender and class
hierarchies, describes *Quadrille* as a confrontation of the
'highly codified, highly restricted, deeply conservative world' of
equestrian sport. There have been three versions of *Quadrille*:
an original 1974 installation at the Women's Free Alliance; the
live performance in Southampton; and an installation at Tate
comprising the documentation of the day's events.

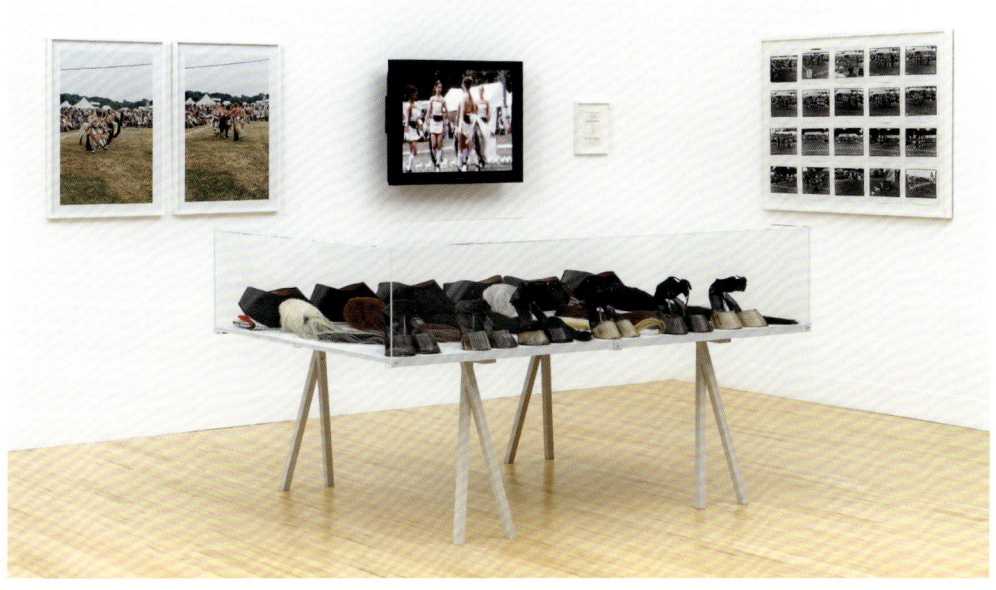

John Everett Millais 1829–96
The New Ride, Kensington Gardens c.1850s
Ink on paper 38 × 50.8 × 2.6

Three young individuals engrossed in conversation ride through Kensington Gardens. All three lean back and pull on the reins; nevertheless, the horses trot forward along a path at which none of them are looking. Rather than making a faithful depiction of a leisurely horse ride, Millais emphasises the way in which the activity facilitates the meeting and connection of these three individuals. Close to the group and to the left, a woman sits side-saddle and talks to her male companion. Rough sketches in the periphery show other groups in conversation or riding. *The New Ride* is part of a series of drawings Millais made in the 1850s to show modern courtship.

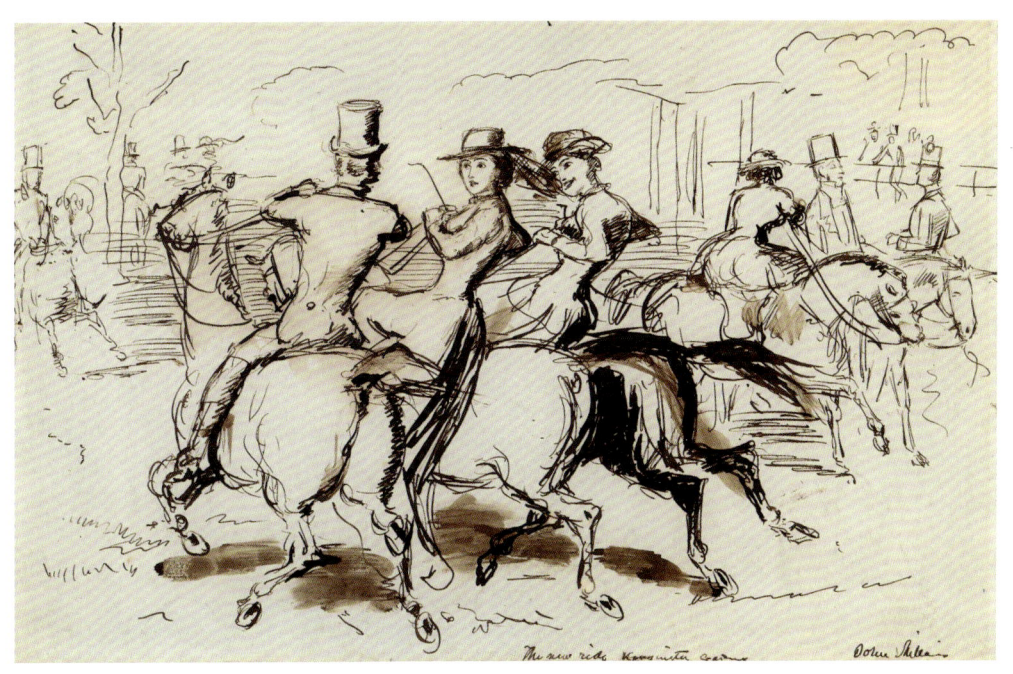

The new ride Kensington Gardens — John Millais

Alfred Munnings 1878–1959
Their Majesties' Return from Ascot 1925
Oil paint on canvas 148 × 244.5

George V, Queen Mary and the future kings Edward VIII and
George VI return to Windsor Castle after attending Ascot
races. Their carriage is pulled by four Windsor Grey horses,
a type selected for use by the British Royal Family at special
occasions for their colour and temperament. The group looks
uniform, the coat on the hindquarters and legs of each horse
marked by black dappling. Only the horse in the back on the
right has a black mane. Two postilion riders in livery are
mounted on the near horses, guiding the animals who pull the
carriage by means of a rig attached to their necks. Munnings
painted the horses and carriage outside from life.

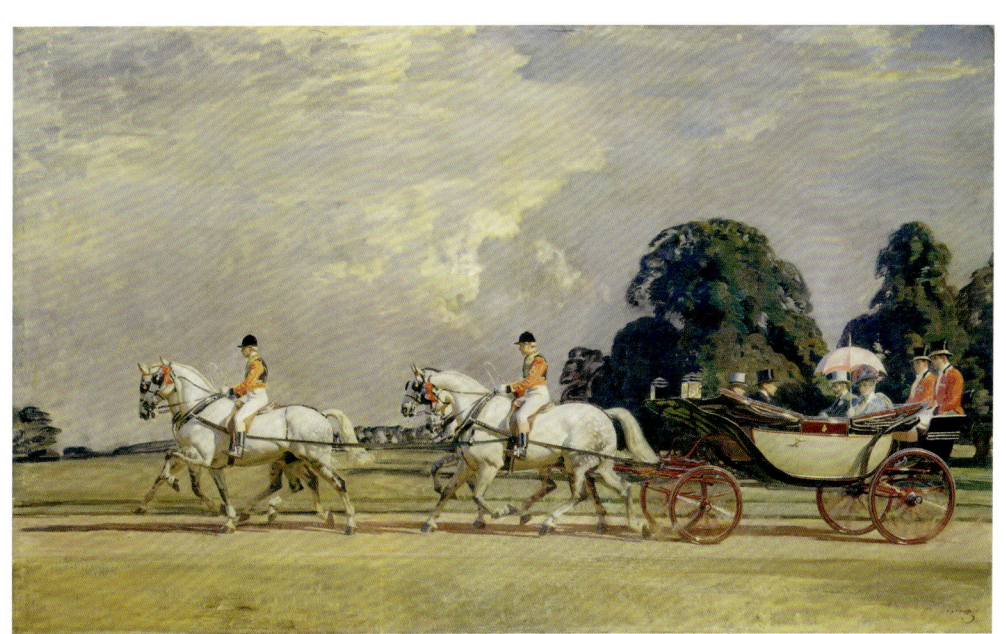

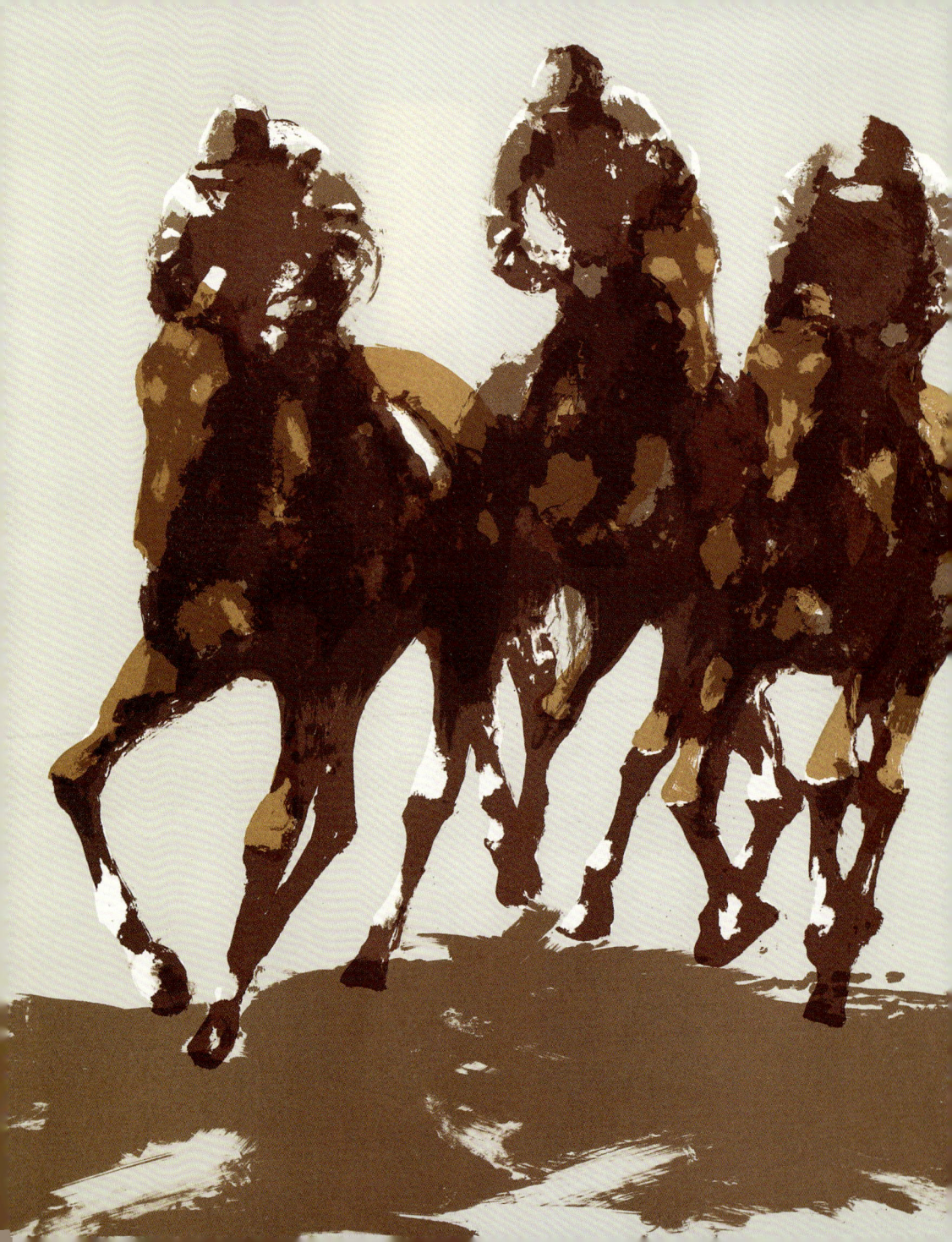

Racing

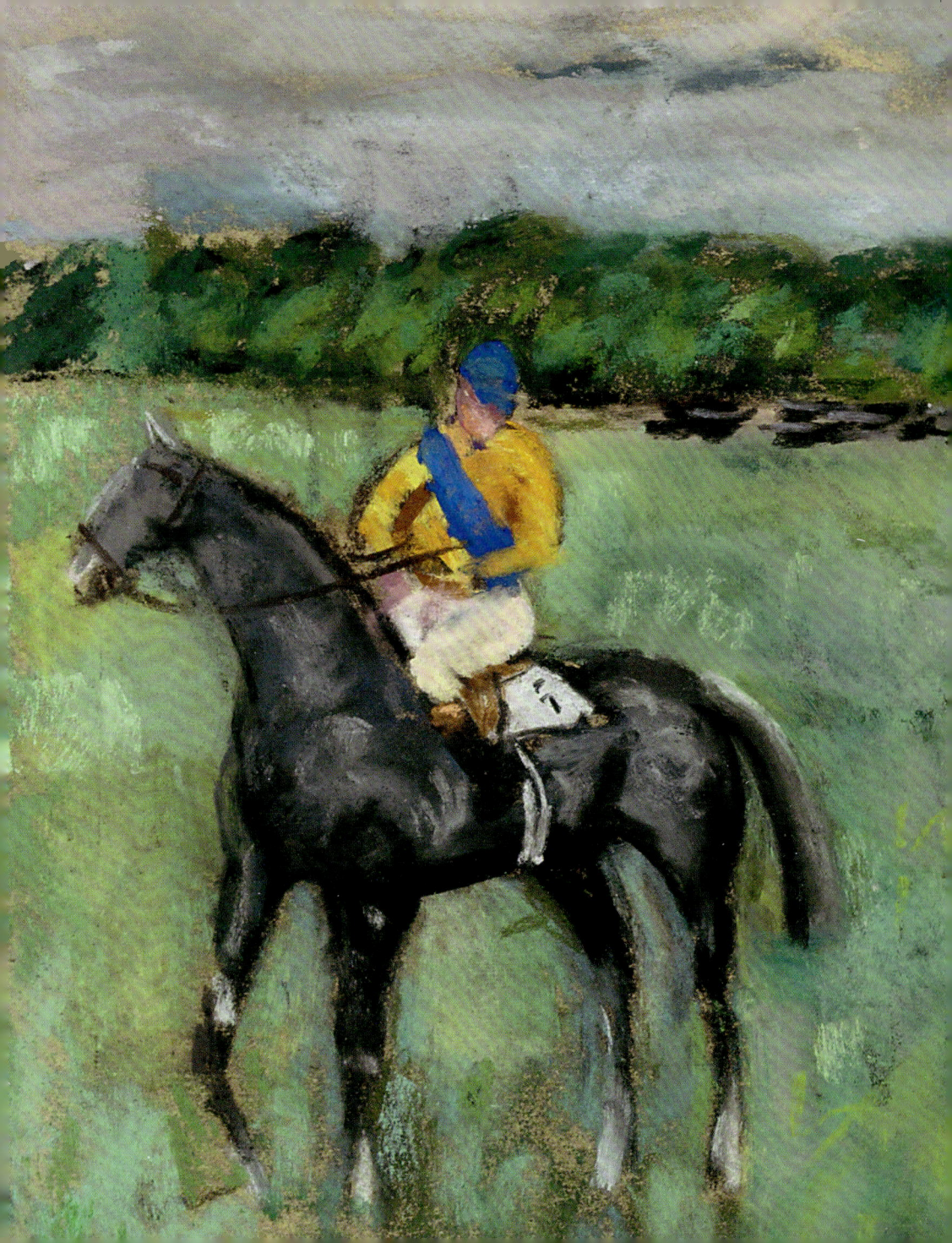

Of all equestrian leisure pursuits, mounted horse-racing is one of the longest standing and most prestigious. The racecourse tests the agility and athleticism of both horse and rider, and success brings glamour, praise and prize money. In the seventeenth and eighteenth centuries, horse-racing became synonymous with lineage and the art of selectively crossing an Arabian stallion with an English mare to create a family tree of successful horses that epitomised speed and power. This Thoroughbred mirrors aristocratic identity, standing in for the owner's supposedly superior bloodline. The Thoroughbred's portrait, which captured its physical likeness and perceived personality, was such a source of pride that it hung in some drawing rooms as an equal to family portraits. Racing is the most egalitarian of equestrian sport, enjoyed by all social classes, and the racing picture conveys the conventions of the sport, its organisation, support, high status and prominence in British culture. Artists translate the hum of spectator chatter into visual form, and show how the unique colour combinations of silk worn by British jockeys during races energise the green of the racetrack. The electric tension in the seconds before the start of a race, when horse and rider brace themselves for a surge forward, becomes palpable through the canvas.

George Stubbs 1724–1806
Otho, with John Larkin up 1768
Oil paint on canvas 101.3 × 127

Stubbs immortalised the winning Thoroughbred racehorse Otho
in this oil painting. The setting is the Newmarket racecourse
where Otho had his greatest success. The bay stands under a
grey, moody sky: there is tension in the atmosphere and Otho's
ears are alert and pricked. These dramatic elements elevate
Stubbs's painting above conventional equine portraiture. Otho's
powerful frame highlights the slenderness of the jockey, John
Larkin. It is not known whether Larkin rode Otho on each
successful occasion, as jockeys' names were not recorded in the
eighteenth century. Stubbs was commissioned to paint this a
year after the end of Otho's racing career. The Thoroughbred
retired to stud in Bedfordshire, breeding a successive generation
of racing horses.

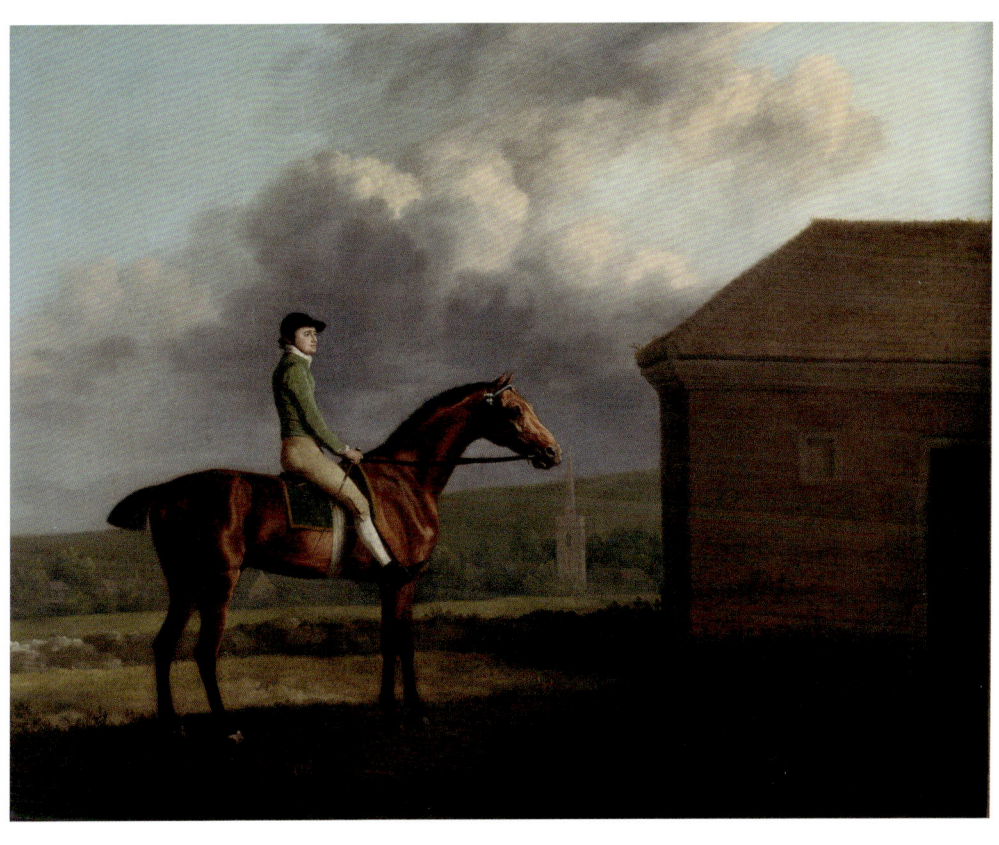

Mark Wallinger born 1959
Half-Brother (Exit to Nowhere – Machiavellian) 1994–5
Oil paint on canvas 230 × 300 × 3.5

This hybrid racehorse is one of four in a series of monumental
paintings. Pairs of horses are painted in thin oil paints on two
white canvases and joined in the middle, making hybrids that
are deliberately incongruous. Here, the front of a bay with a
roached (trimmed) mane is paired with the rear of a glossy black
horse. Wallinger used translucent glazes to achieve a very high
gloss on the bodies. The images of the horses are taken from
the Jockey Club's official record of Thoroughbred stallions.
'Half-brother' is a term in racing denoting horses that have the
same mother. A stallion can mate with dozens of mares in a season,
whilst a brood mare will have just one foal. The progeny of great
mares are therefore rarer and more valuable. The broodmare
Coup de Folie was the dam of both horses depicted here.

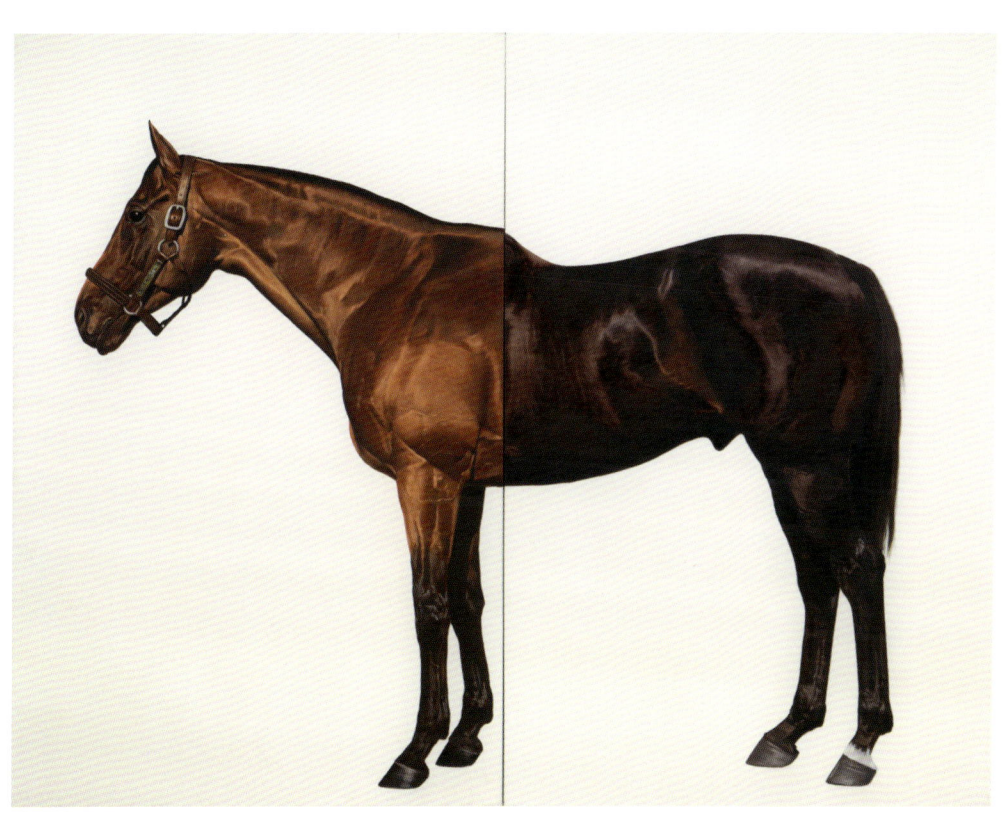

William Roberts 1895–1980
Cantering to the Post 1949
Oil paint on canvas 61 × 50.8

Three horses and their riders race to the finish line. All six
figures are depicted in a stylised manner, with compact bodies,
simple lines and colours that harmonise. The scene is stripped
of an audience and expansive track, focusing attention on just
these three contenders. They are grouped tightly together in
an almost square fashion. The riders look down in concentration
as they drive their steeds forward, while the horses look up,
mouths open and ears pricked, clearly alert and straining
towards the finish line. They appear to be flying, each seeming
to be hovering a few centimetres above the ground.

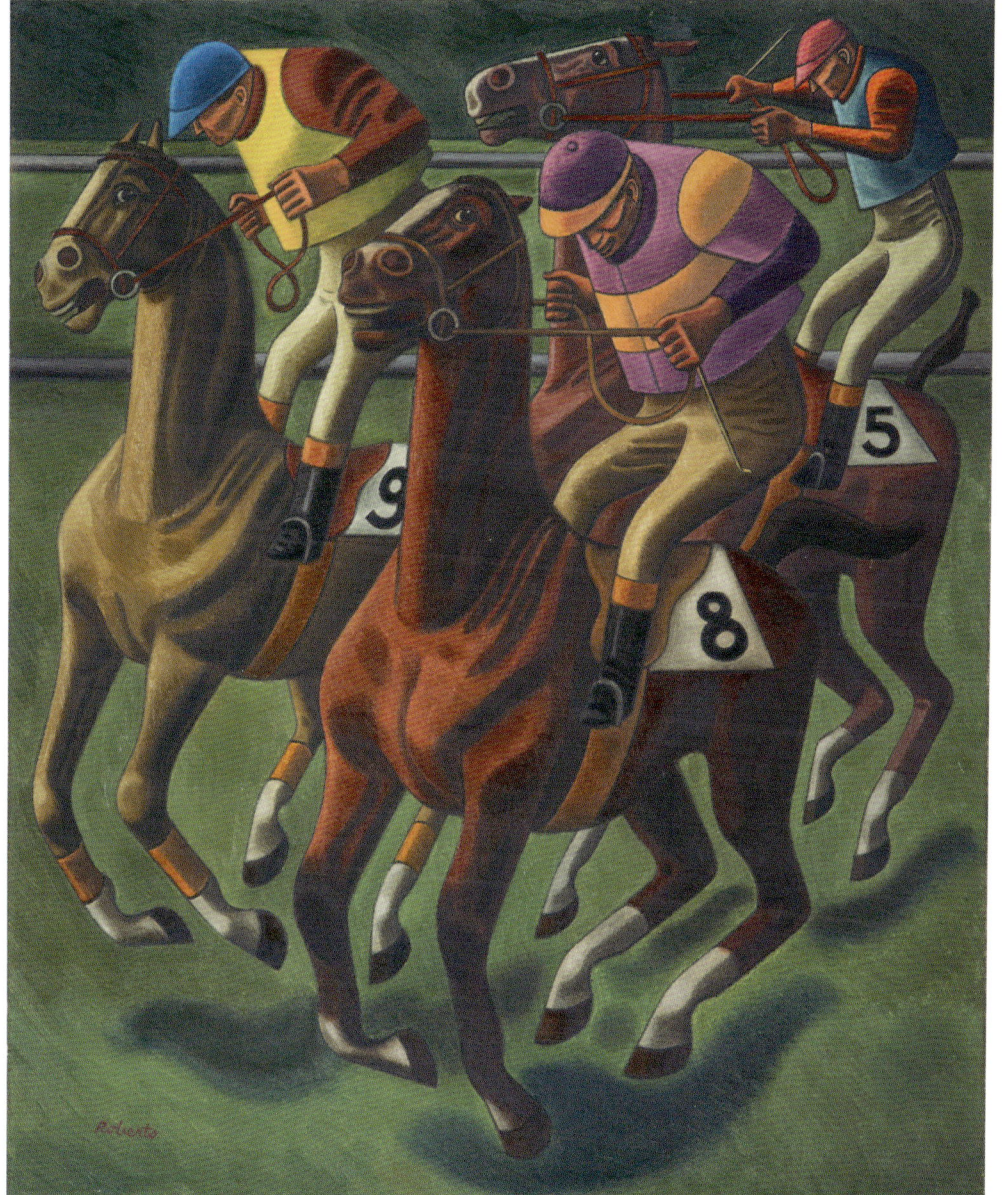

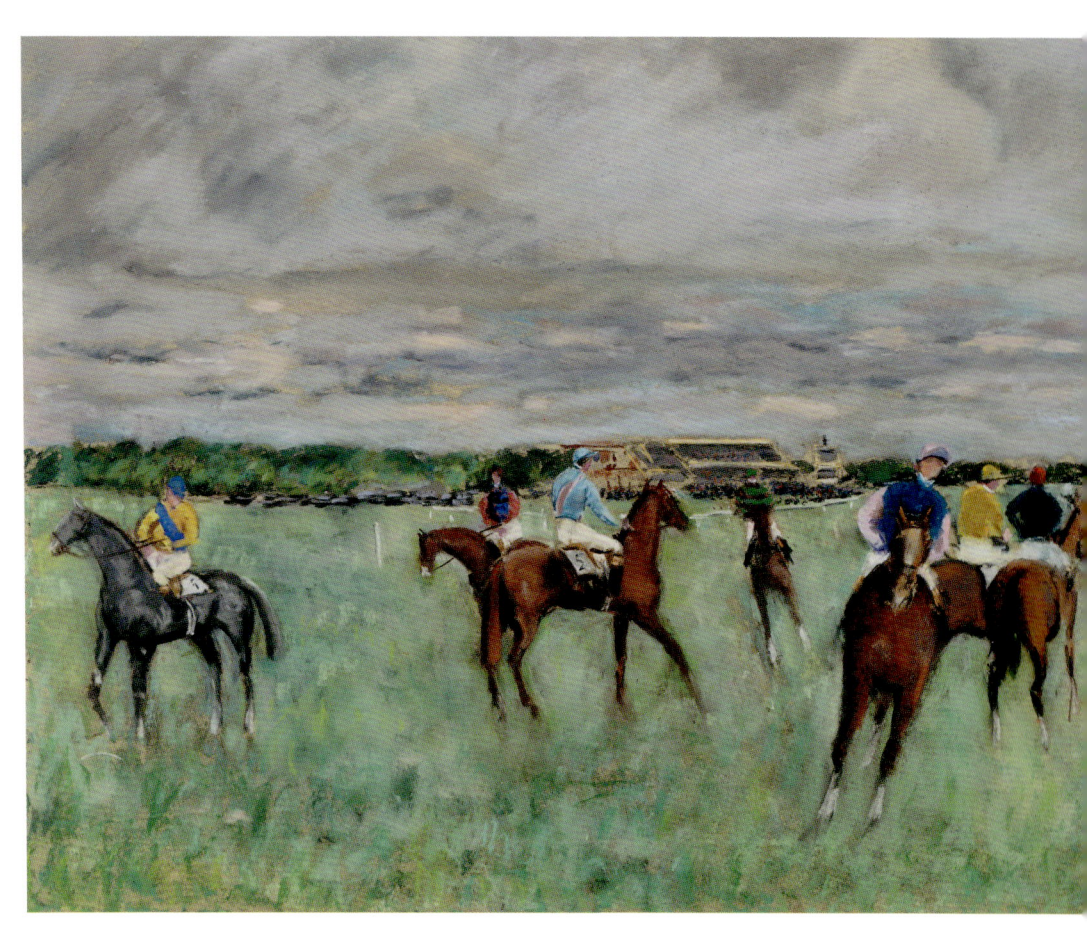

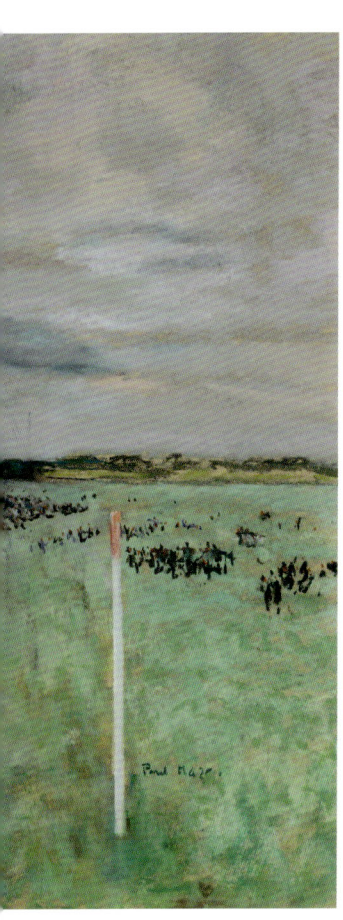

Paul Maze 1887–1979
The Rowley Mile, Newmarket 1929
Pastel on paper 35.5 × 70

Maze depicted a group of horses and their riders on the Rowley
Mile, one of the two racecourses at Newmarket. It is likely they
are milling around before the start of the race, at a time before
the introduction of starting stalls. Spectators gather on the
grass on the right hand side, coming up to see the horses as they
go off; others assemble in the background by the grandstand
where the race will finish. The second jockey from the left wears
the purple and scarlet of the royal silks, colours that have been
worn by jockeys riding in the name of King George VI, Queen
Elizabeth II and King Charles III. Rowley Mile has been raced on
since the seventeenth century and is named after King Charles
II's favourite stallion, Old Rowley.

Peter Howell born 1932
The Last Furlong 1973
Lithograph on paper 48.3 × 70.5

Three horses and their jockeys gallop at full speed towards the viewer, striving for the win, their shadows blending into one. This is the last furlong, meaning that the finish line is in sight, no more than two hundred metres away. Howell's use of shades of brown on the jockeys' silks and coats of the horse focuses the attention on the action. The jockeys lean forward, their bodies compact over the horses, keeping as still as possible as they grip at the reins just behind the horses' necks. Their bottoms float over the saddle to absorb the ups and downs of the animals' motion, and the burden of their weight rests on their legs, not the horses' backs. Both horse and rider are athletes.

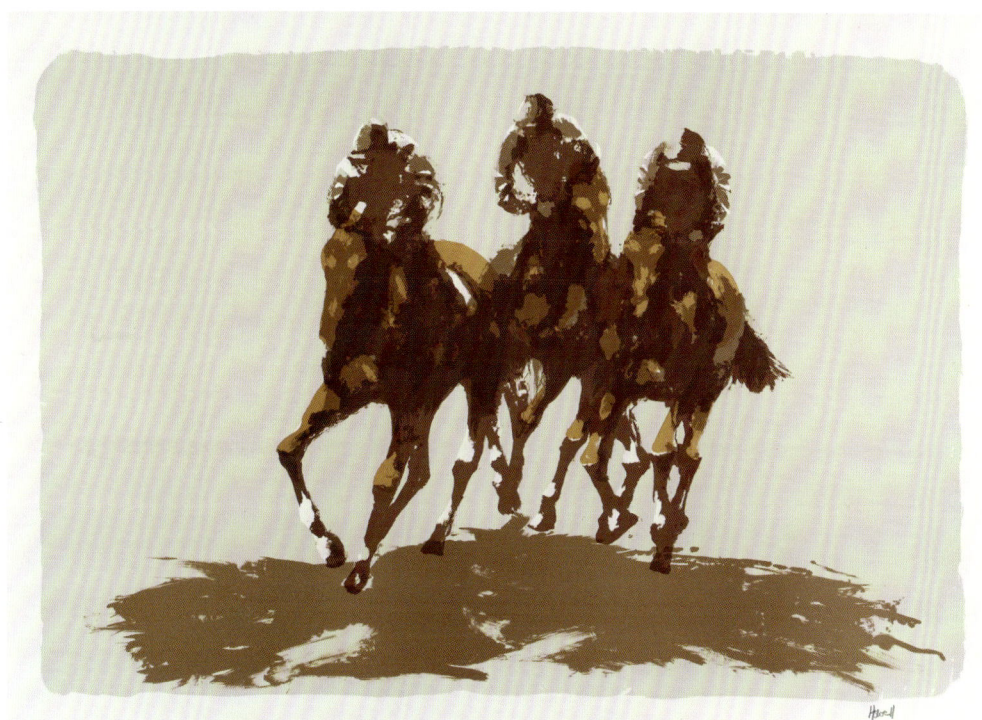

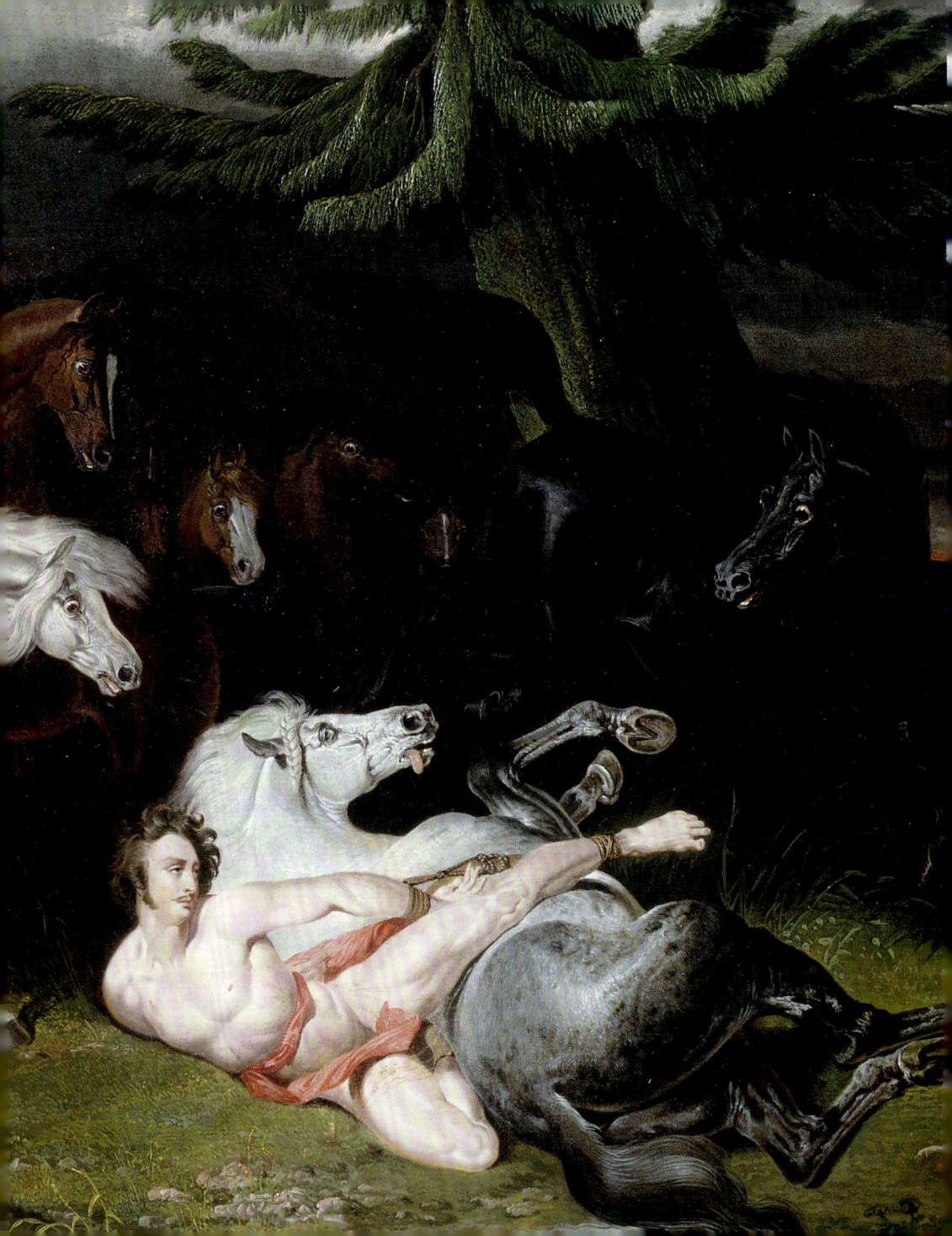

Literature

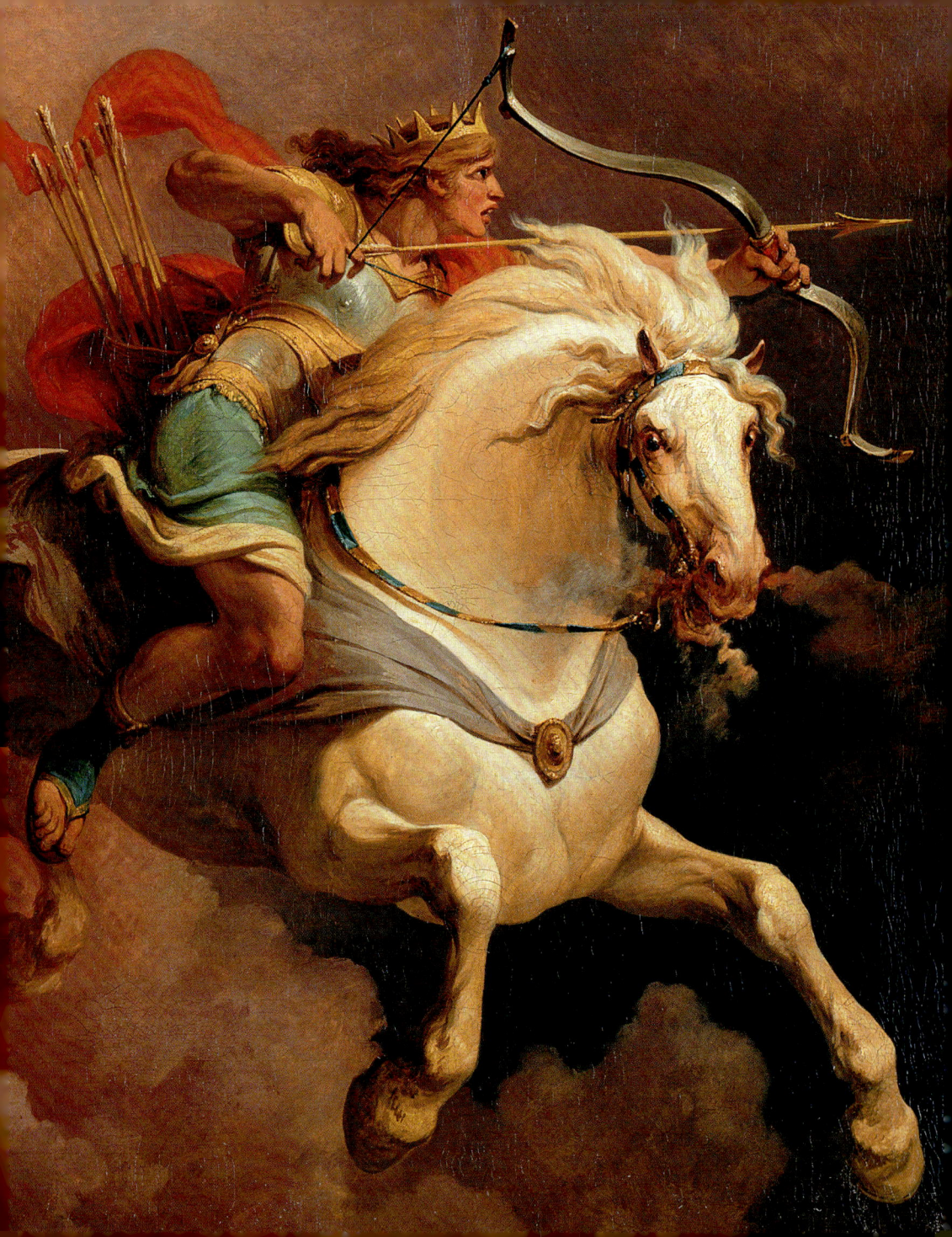

A writer chooses words in a novel as deliberately as a visual artist chooses the colour, medium and scale of their work. Both literature and visual art draw a reader in, inspire thought, evoke experiences, entertain and soothe. Both are revelatory. In the words of sculptor and printmaker Dame Elisabeth Frink, the value of all the arts is 'to make people aware of all sorts of different areas of their minds.' In both literature and visual art, horses signify chivalry, freedom, movement, ferocity and formidable strength. This symbolism can recall in the reader and viewer's mind wide-ranging aspects of the human experience: debilitating heartbreak, childhood innocence, collective fear, and indiscretions and their punishment. In depicting the words and tales of a wordsmith, an artist provides another way of recalling these experiences, applying their skill in painting, printmaking and collage to the writer's world.

Barnett Freedman 1901–58
Untitled. Verso: The Real Spring had Come 1950
Part of *Illustrations for 'Anna Karenina' I–XIV*
Lithograph on paper 96.8 × 62.9

Levin, the fictional landowner from Leo Tolstoy's nineteenth-
century novel *Anna Karenina* (1878), rides his 'good little horse',
Kolpik. He is full of new energy after a winter spent ruminating
over a rejected marriage proposal. Freedman illustrates the
moment Levin leaves the forest and enters an immense plain.
Tolstoy wrote: 'The further he rode, the happier he became, and
plans for the land rose to his mind each better than the last'.
The horizontal washes in the foreground and trees, and the
horse's mane and tail blowing in the wind, indicate Levin's speed.
He appears relaxed in this new season, his forward trajectory
on the horse a symbol of his healing heart and future plans. In
Tolstoy's words, 'the real spring had come.'

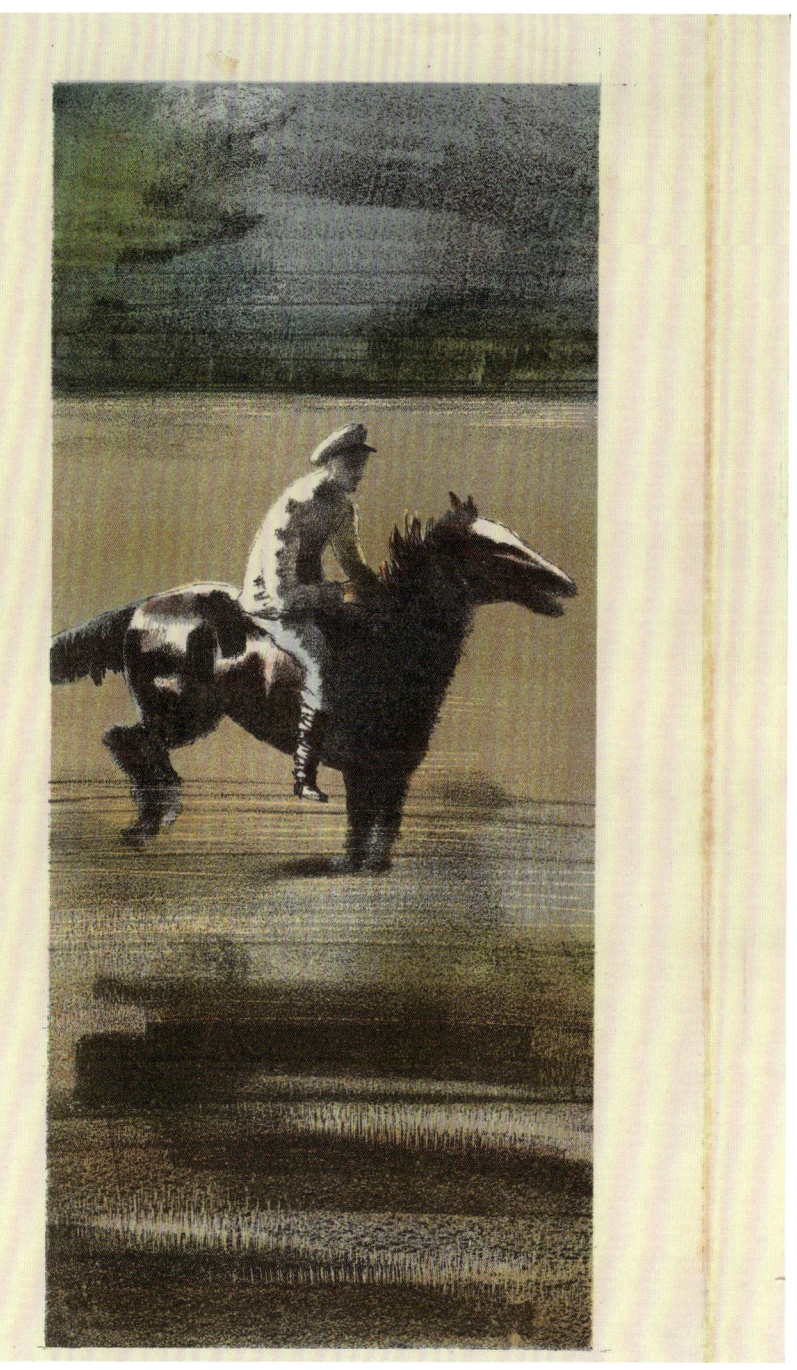

Dame Elisabeth Frink 1930–93
The Knight's Tale 1972
Part of Chaucer's *'Canterbury Tales'*
Etching and aquatint on paper 49.7 × 34.5

'The Knight's Tale' is the first story in Geoffrey Chaucer's *Canterbury Tales* (c.1400). Frink illustrates the moment when one of the protagonists – Theseus, the Duke of Athens, 'in all felicity and height of pride' – is stopped by a group of widowed women dressed in black, 'each pair, in proper station, / Behind the other.' Theseus and his horse are in a white, negative space, while the sky, landscape and the women are depicted in dark aquatint, a variety of complex printmaking techniques creating the textured effect on the paper. Theseus's facial features are the clearest: his chiselled jaw, visible in profile (and his muscled body), reflect classical notions of beauty. With his imposing stature amplified by the horse, Theseus embodies the idea of chivalry. In Chaucer's story, Theseus goes on to imprison two of the knights linked to the slain men.

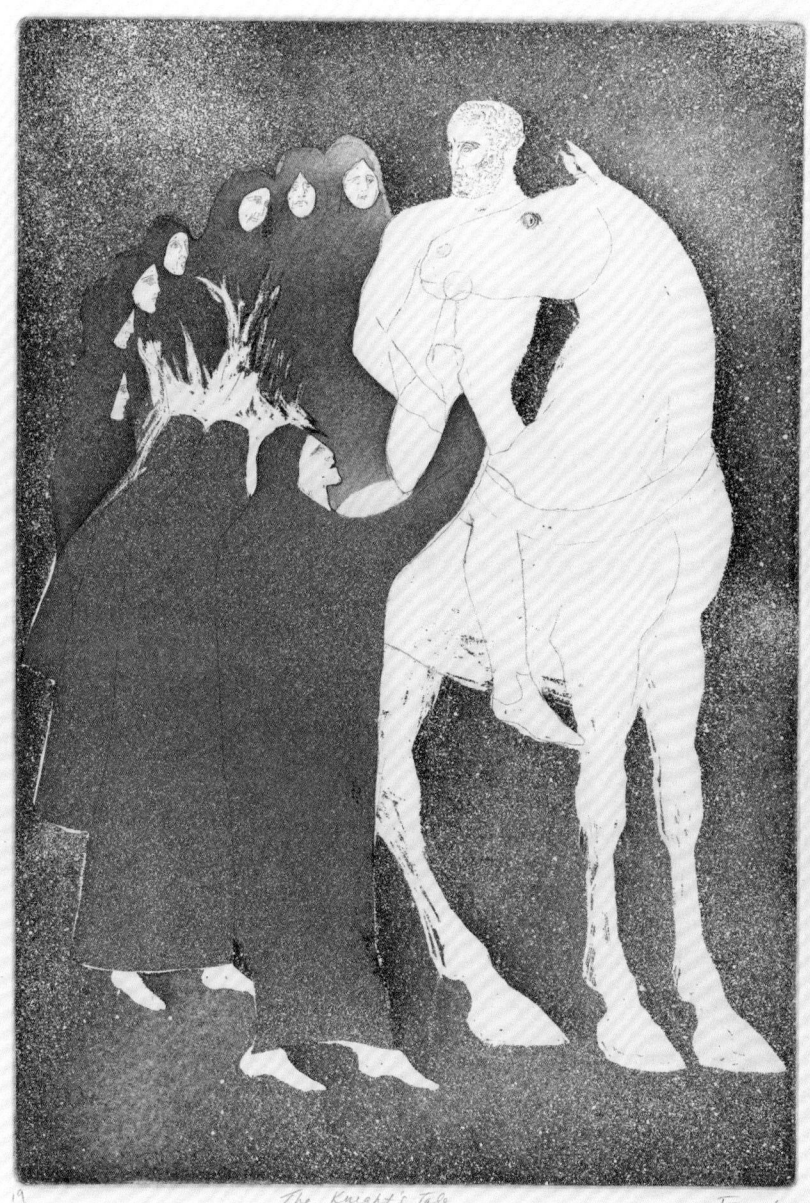

The Knight's Tale

Frink

John Frederick Herring 1795–1865
Mazeppa Surrounded by Horses (after Horace Vernet) c.1833
Oil paint on canvas 55.9 × 76.2

Mazeppa, written by the Romantic poet Lord Byron in 1819,
became a source for Romantic painters. The poem is based on
a legend featuring a Ukrainian military leader of the same name,
and tells how the youthful Mazeppa embarks on a love affair
with a countess whose husband, discovering this illicit liaison,
punishes Mazeppa by tying him naked to a wild horse described
in the poem as a 'noble steed, / A Tartar of the Ukraine breed'.
The count then lets them loose in the wilderness. Herring's
nocturnal scene shows the dramatic moment when Mazeppa
and the horse have fallen at the foot of a large fir tree. Other
horses gallop into the scene from the left, their faces showing
both fear and curiosity. Herring portrays with precision the
individuality of each animal's emotional expression.

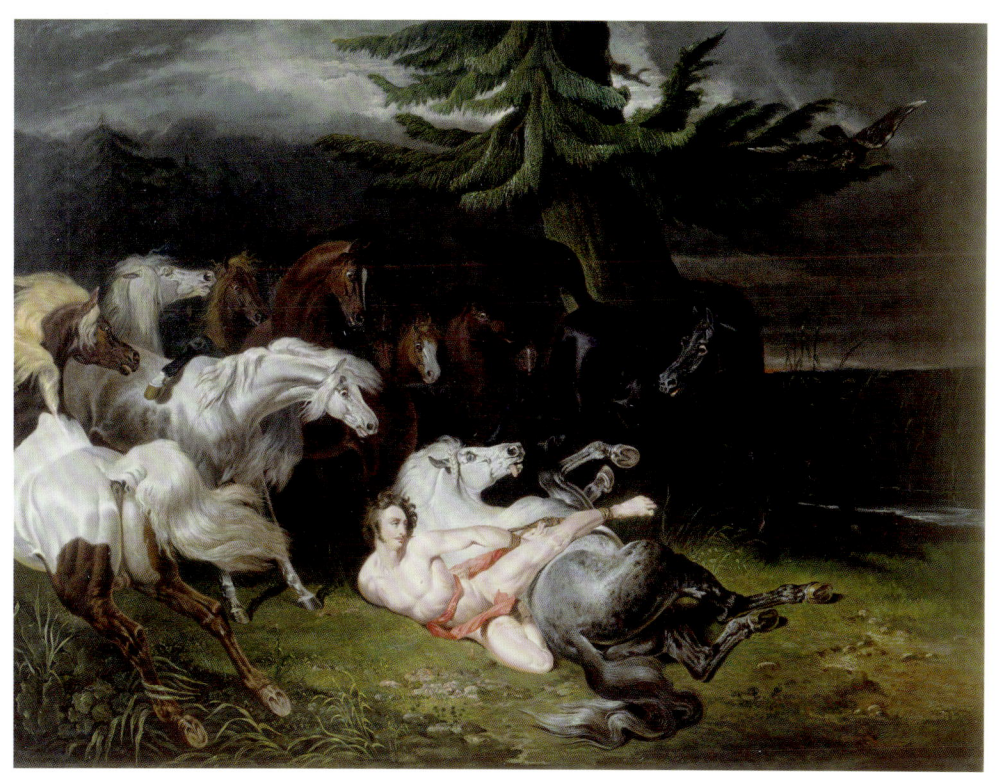

Philip James de Loutherbourg 1740–1812
The Vision of the White Horse 1798
Oil paint on canvas 122.2 × 99.1

The first two of the four horsemen of the Apocalypse, Conquest and War, charge forward in a dramatic cloudscape towards the viewer. Conquest draws his bow, astride a white horse who glares with bloodshot eyes and bares his teeth, mouth gaping. War wields a sword and rides a red horse, the horse's colour barely visible in the angry, nebulous glow. The riders and horses symbolise total devastation and disaster. Apocalyptic subjects increasingly appeared in the visual culture of the last decade of the eighteenth century, a time marked by the French Revolution, the global reach of the consequent wars, and fears of the approaching millennium. Loutherbourg painted this for London print-seller Thomas Macklin's Bible Gallery, a commercial gallery featuring paintings of Biblical subjects. His contribution combined his artistic and spiritual interests.

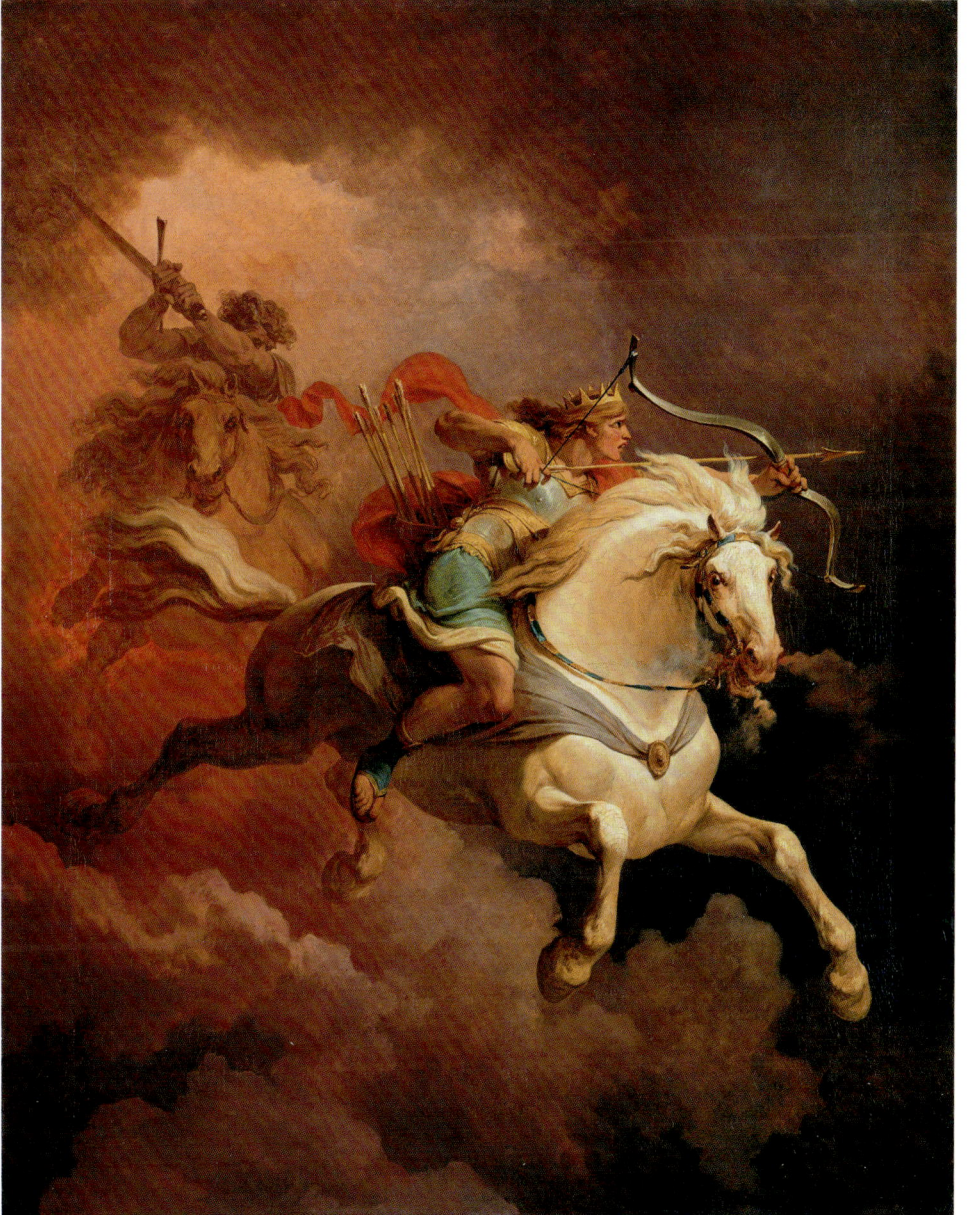

Peter Blake born 1932
'and the two knights sat and looked at each
other without speaking' 1970
Screenprint on paper 24.3 × 18.1

Blake's print depicts a scene from the eighth chapter of Lewis
Carroll's *Through the Looking-Glass* (1871). Here, Alice comes
across the Red Knight as he is riding through the wood. He
attempts to imprison her, before the White Knight comes to
the rescue. The two sit atop their horses, staring wordlessly
at one another, until a furious fight results in the defeat of the
Red Knight. On their ensuing journey together, the White Knight
describes to Alice the inventions in his possession. The forms
in Blake's print are unclear but, as described in the original
story, the knight carries a beehive, helmet and mousetrap, while
the chunky grey anklets he wears guard against shark bites.
Both of Blake's horses are stylised, distorting our perception
of the two knights' statures and the forest beyond.

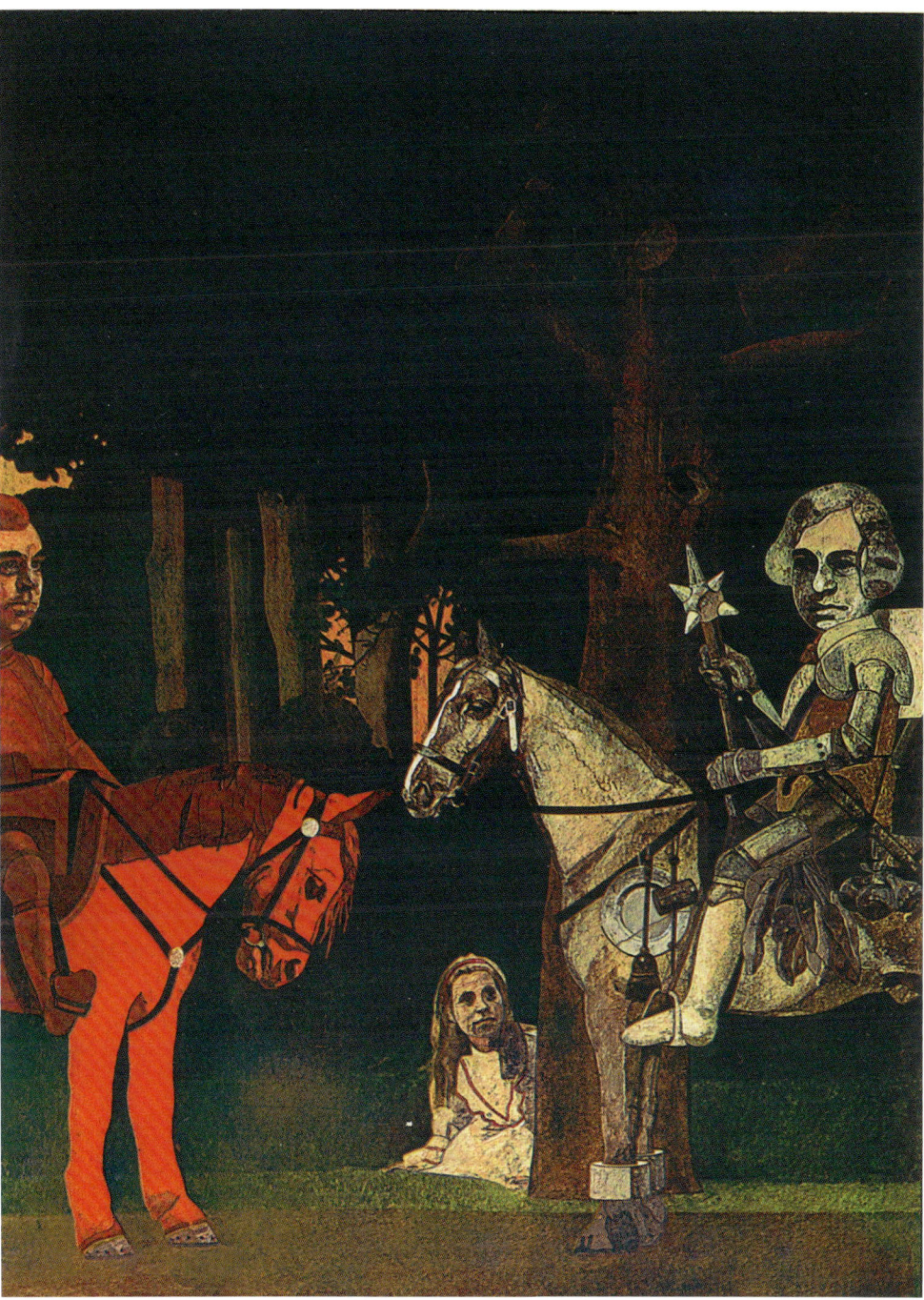

William Blake 1757–1827
Pity c.1795
Colour print, ink and watercolour on paper 42.5 × 53.9

This scene is inspired by William Shakespeare's play *Macbeth*, first performed c.1606. When the titular character is debating whether to murder King Duncan, he envisages the pity that will be felt for the King. His metaphor for pity is a 'naked new-born babe' that spreads the sad news while riding the wind or on invisible horses. In Blake's image, the baby springs up from their motionless mother to an angel riding a 'sightless' horse. Behind them is another horse and rider. Blake's linear style creates a fluidity that results in the horses and riders appearing almost as a single being. The angel facing us needs not steer, for the horse intuitively knows the direction.

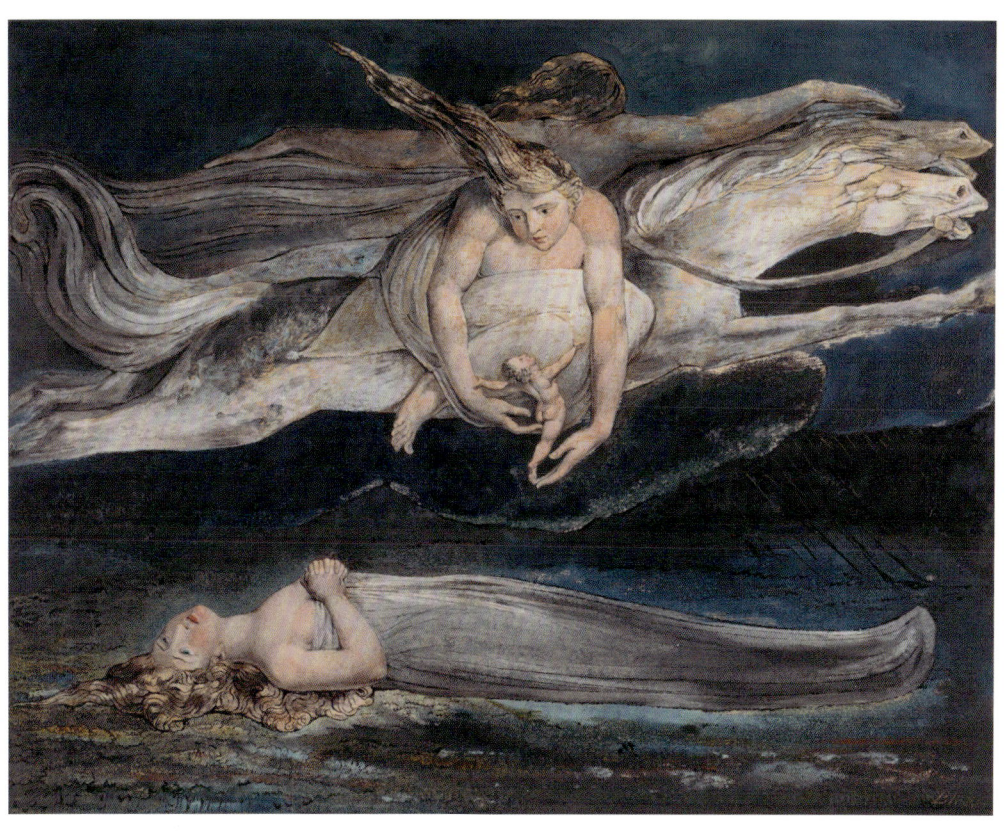

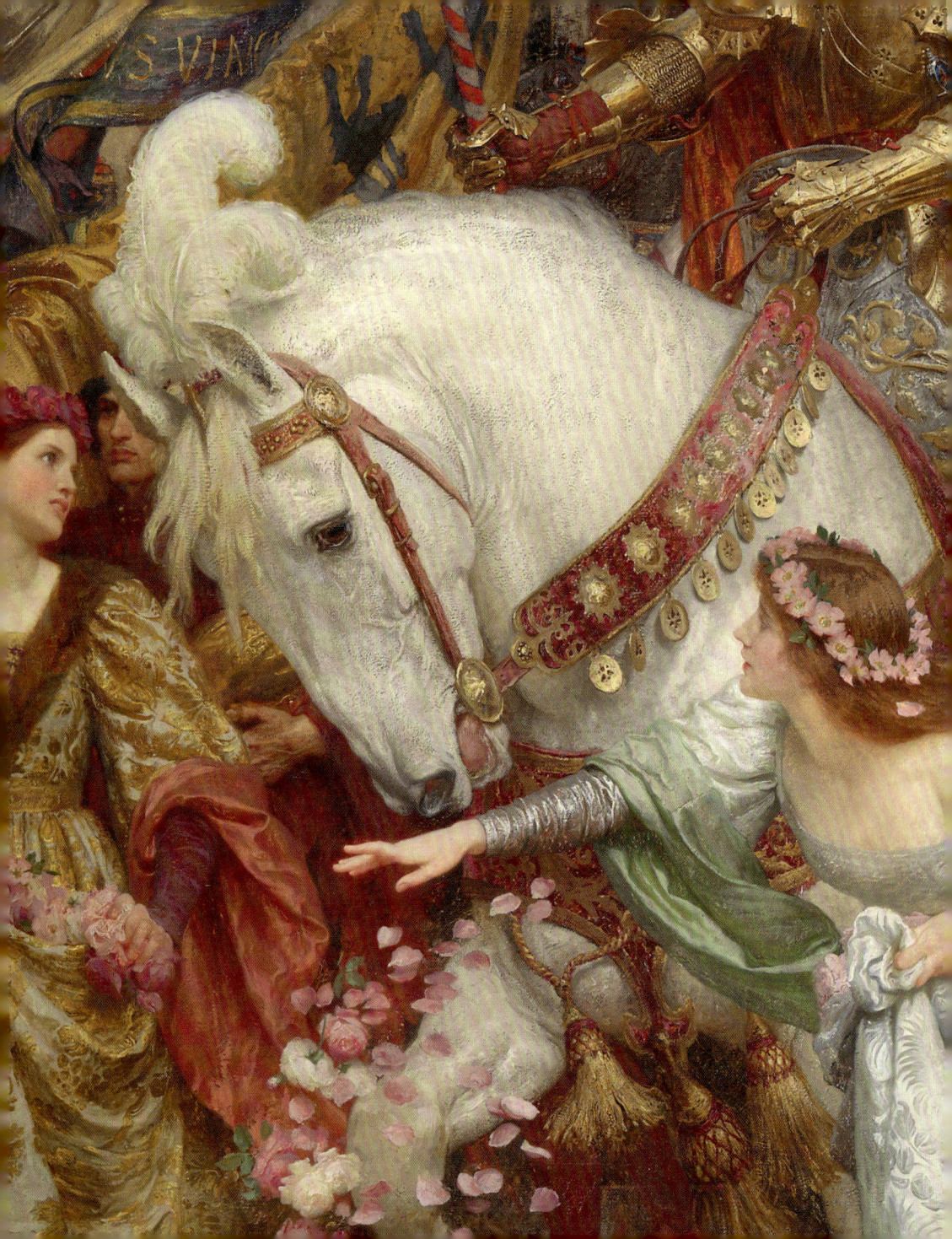

Human
Imagination

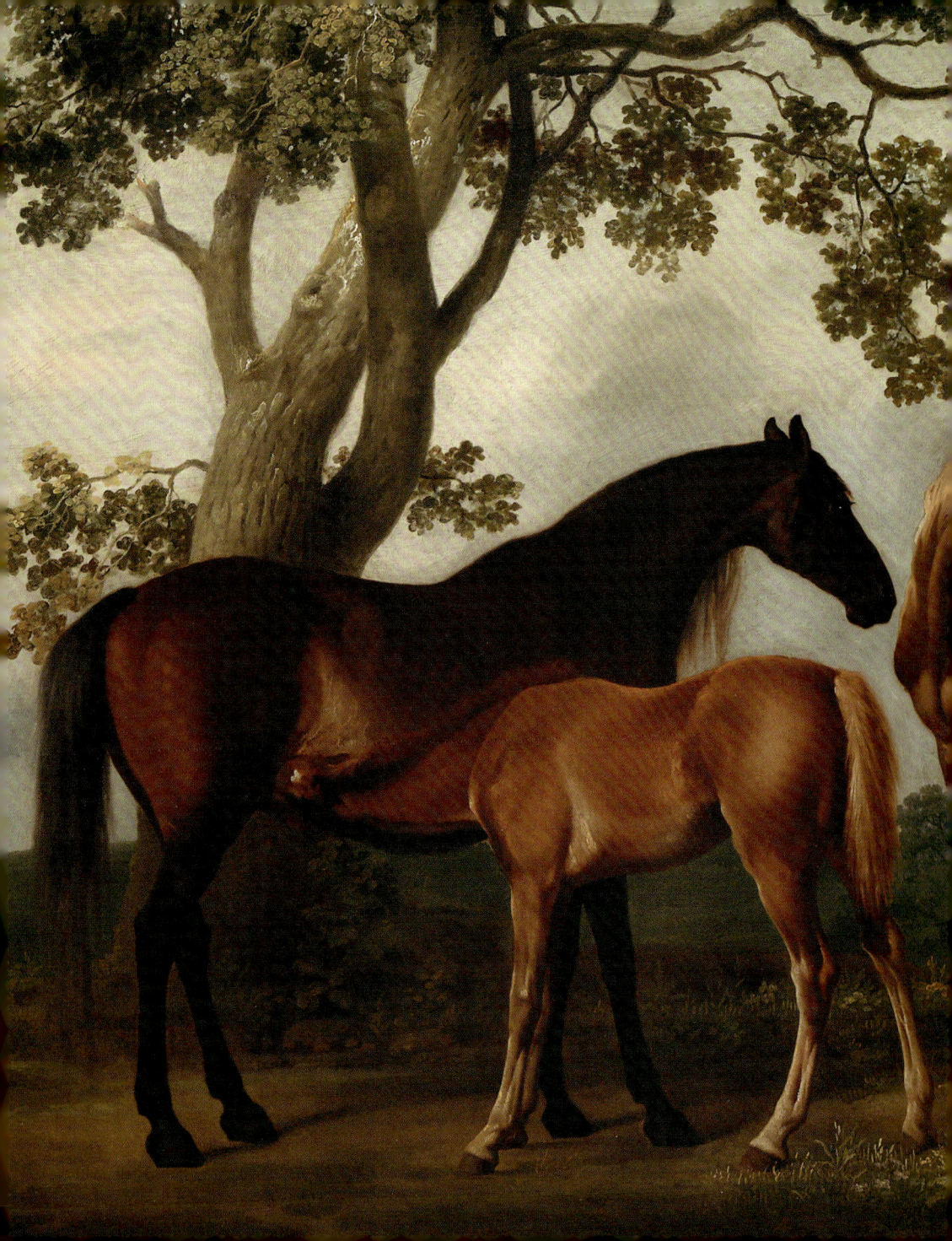

British art has been marked by the symbolism of the horse – its strength, nobility, heroism, triumph, speed, industriousness, mystery and splendour. At first in eighteenth-century visual culture, the horse was a humble subject. In dissecting horses, George Stubbs sought to understand them anatomically before visualising them with precision and detail, revolutionising and valorising the aesthetic and scientific representation of the horse. Stubbs and other artists of the eighteenth century ascribed human emotion to their horse imagery to elicit the feelings necessary for their visual narratives. This sentimentality conjures up a world free of strife, conflict or competition. To the Romantic artists of the nineteenth century, the idealised beauty of the horse, its air of mystery and esteemed position in the natural world suited their artistic movement. Some later artists favoured the artistic expression of the horse's physicality and impressive stature; for others, it is a desire to represent the essence of the horse that lingers. With abstraction, the horse becomes untethered from its historical connections to labour, racing, transportation and war. New forms of expression become possible. The inquisitive mind remains captivated by the horse, both its nature and depiction in art.

George Stubbs, *Mares and Foals in a River Landscape* c.1763–8 (detail, see p.142)

Frank Dicksee 1853–1928
The Two Crowns 1900
Oil paint on canvas 231.1 × 182.3

A large white Spanish-type horse decorated with three feathers triumphantly carries a knight through an adoring crowd. The knight wears dazzling armour and a gold crown, and looks up transfixed at the cross-bearing Christ with his crown of thorns. Its dry jaggedness is in stark contrast to the knight's own opulent headpiece, and reminds him of the brevity of his earthly riches, fame and power – that he is mortal. The knight's spiritual awakening has begun. There is, however, a chance for his redemption. The whiteness of the horse, and its associations with purity and transformation, is a counterpoint to the riotous colours of the banners, balcony tapestry and women's richly decorated dresses. In Dicksee's highly moralising scene, the white horse can carry the knight away from the trappings of success.

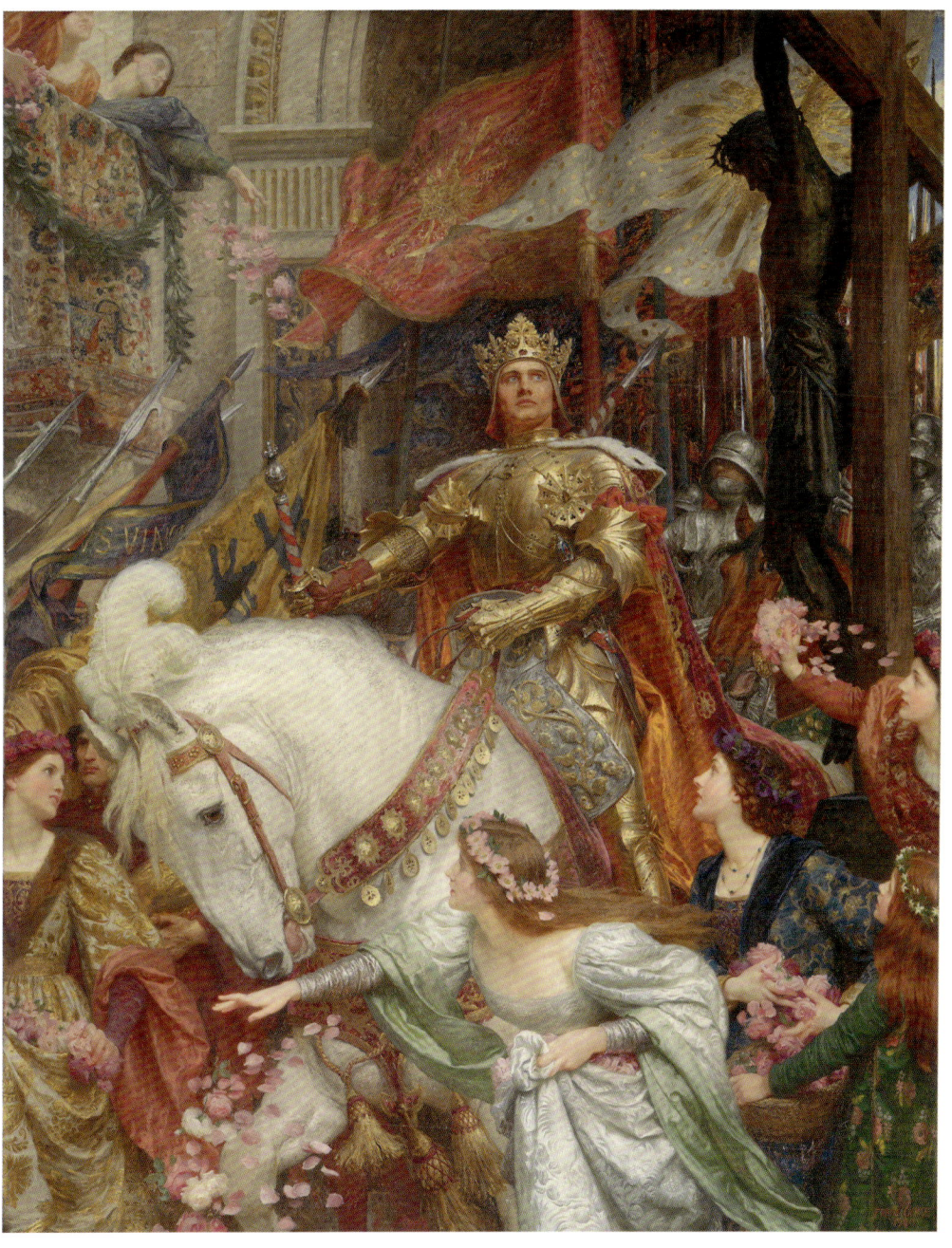

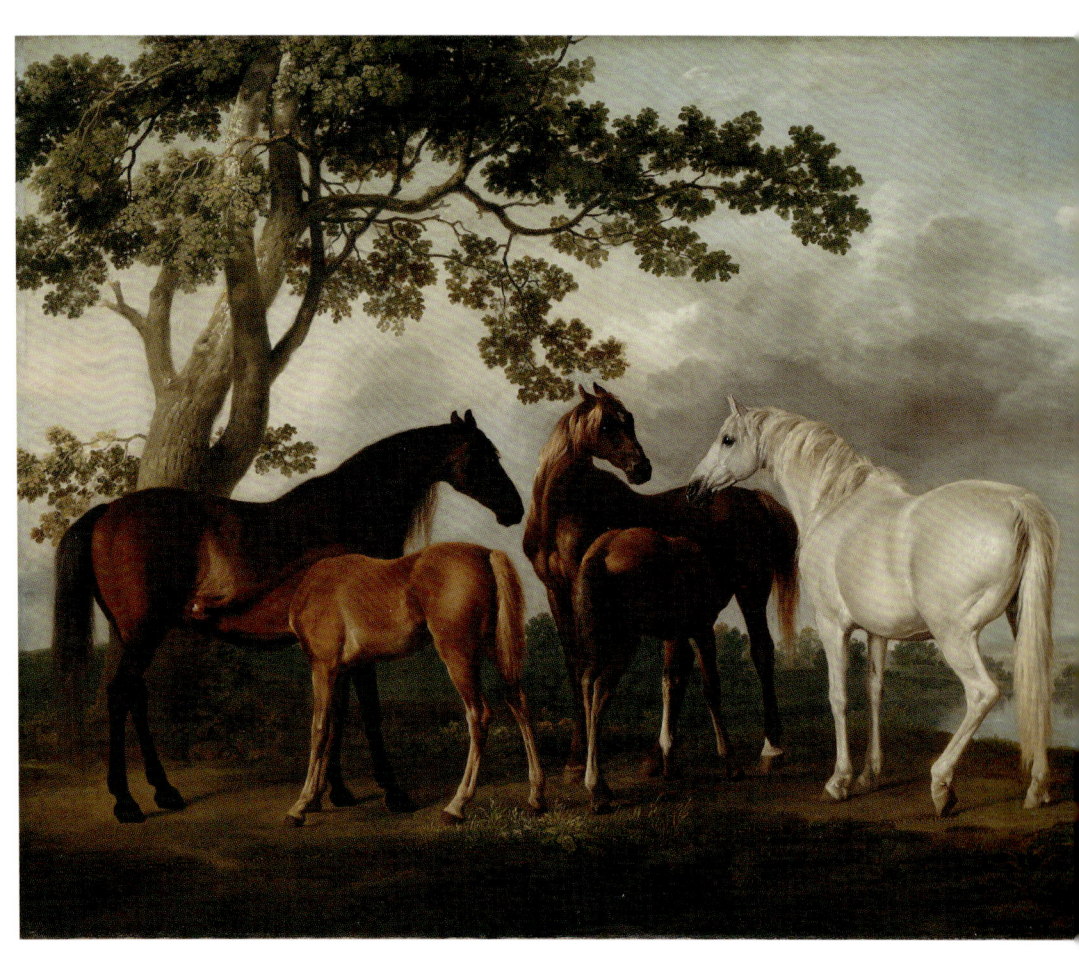

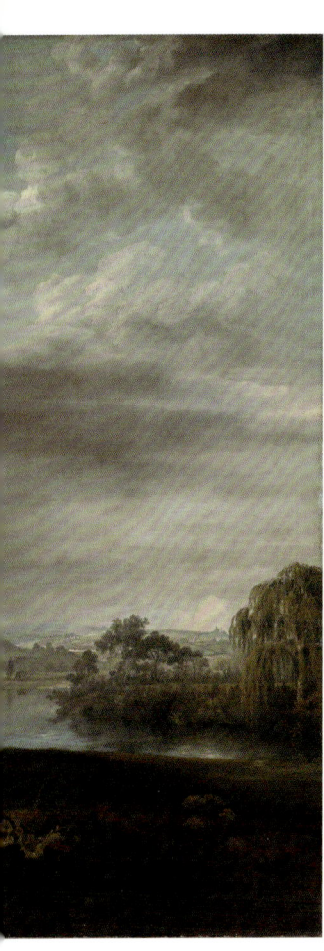

George Stubbs 1724–1806
Mares and Foals in a River Landscape c.1763–8
Oil paint on canvas 101.6 × 161.9

Brood mares and their foals gather under the cover of a huge
tree in what is possibly an imagined landscape. The mares are
based on specific mares who had birthed winning racehorses
or had themselves achieved racing success. This scene is a more
intimate mode of commemorating important horses, one of
Stubbs's most popular subjects, and the artist created nearly
a dozen variations on this theme for his patrons. There is
symmetry and balance to the group: the three heads of the
mares come together and create a focal point within the
composition, while Stubbs positions the rumps of the bay and
the grey so they form the edge of the group. The naturalism
of their bodies stems from Stubbs's meticulous study of the
anatomy of the horse. This adds to the perceived naturalism
of what is a carefully arranged scene.

John Frederick Herring 1795–1865
The Frugal Meal exhibited 1847
Oil paint on canvas 54.6 × 74.9

Two white ponies and one black one in shadow share a meal
of hay while two birds look on. The horses' heads are closely
grouped, a format that Herring adopted in his paintings in the
1840s. The dark background provides no detail of their location;
they may be in a stable or in a farmyard. The atmosphere
reads as gloomy, but there is a tenderness among the horses.
Herring's title prompts viewers to consider what constitutes
scarcity and abundance. The sense of love and unity the animals
share triumphs over the hardship suggested by the title. Artists
including Pablo Picasso and the Dutch painter Jozef Israëls
have also employed the theme of the 'frugal meal' in their work.

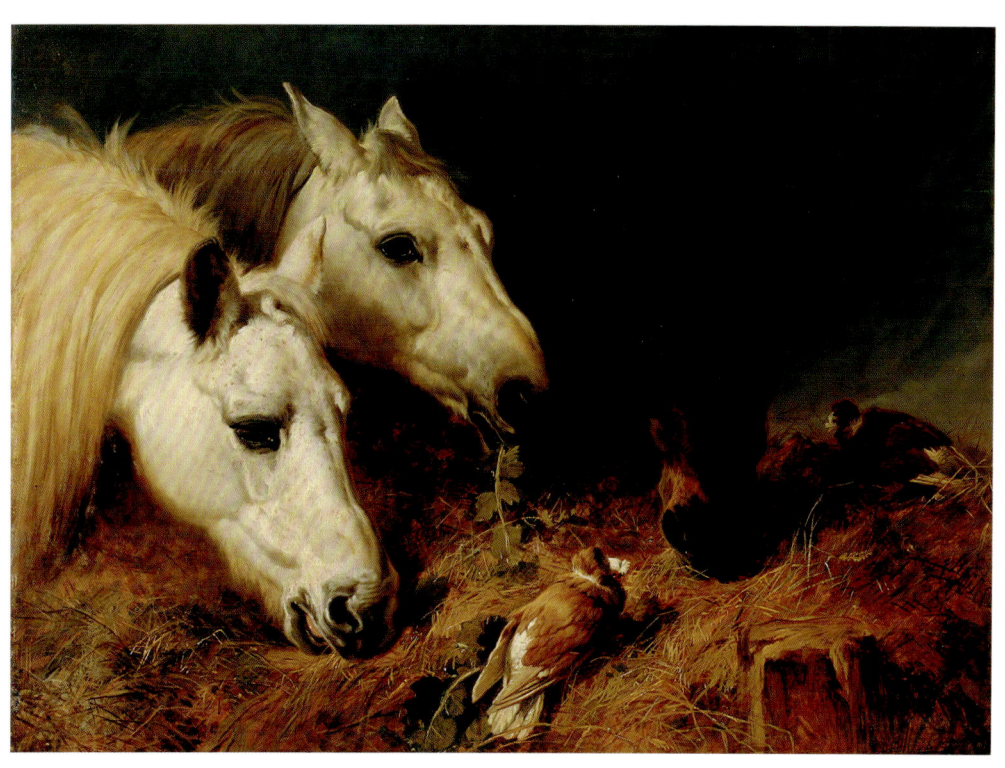

Henry Lamb 1883–1960
Phantasy 1912
Oil paint on canvas 86.4 × 61

Two nude individuals and a white horse occupy the majority
of Lamb's painting. One figure gazes into the distance while
the other occupies themselves with the horse's reins. The pair
will ride bareback as there is no saddle. Their proximity to the
horse, and Lamb's use of similar white-beige tones for the
horse's coat and their skin, signals a deep connection between
human and animal. In the background, a third nude rider and his
horse appear almost as one. The landscape's dusky pink replaces
the earthy browns, greens and grey we might expect. The
subdued palette and subject matter are reminiscent of Pablo
Picasso's *Boy Leading a Horse* 1905–6, painted a few years prior.
In a 1955 letter Lamb remarked that he painted this 'when [he]
was riding a good deal'.

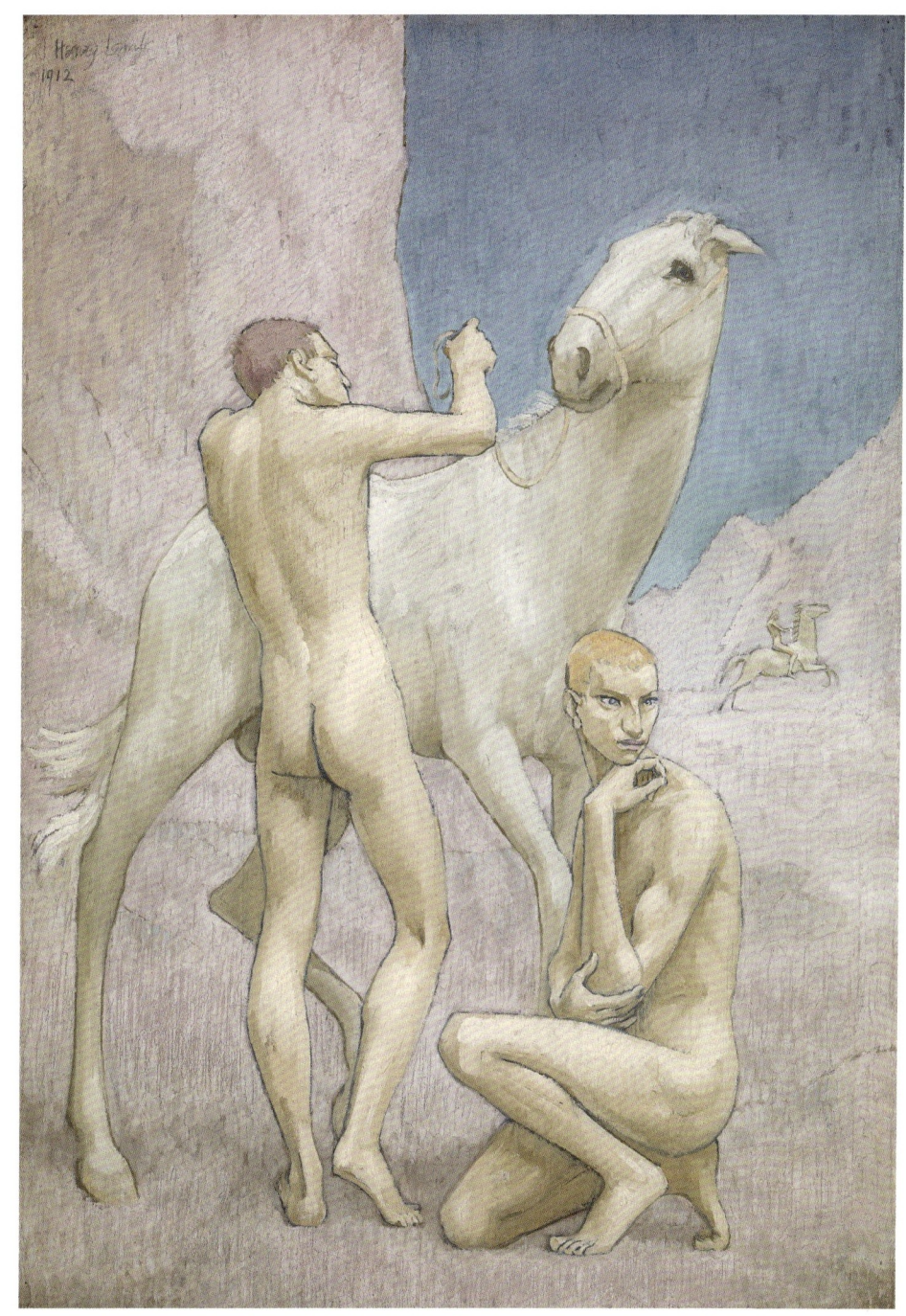

William Roberts 1895–1980
The Horsemen 1920
Watercolour and graphite on paper 15.2 × 18.4

Three horses and their riders pause for conversation, gesturing
animatedly. Although they appear to be in a hilly landscape, very
little of the background is visible. Roberts contains his subjects
within a grid of thirty squares on a section of the page, minimising
most of the peripheral details. The focus is on the interaction
and gestures of the figures and horses. All six bodies are simplified
into forms marked out by straight lines or simple forms, the
diagonals meticulously worked out on the grid. The riders lean
to the left, but their angular outstretched arms give balance
to the composition.

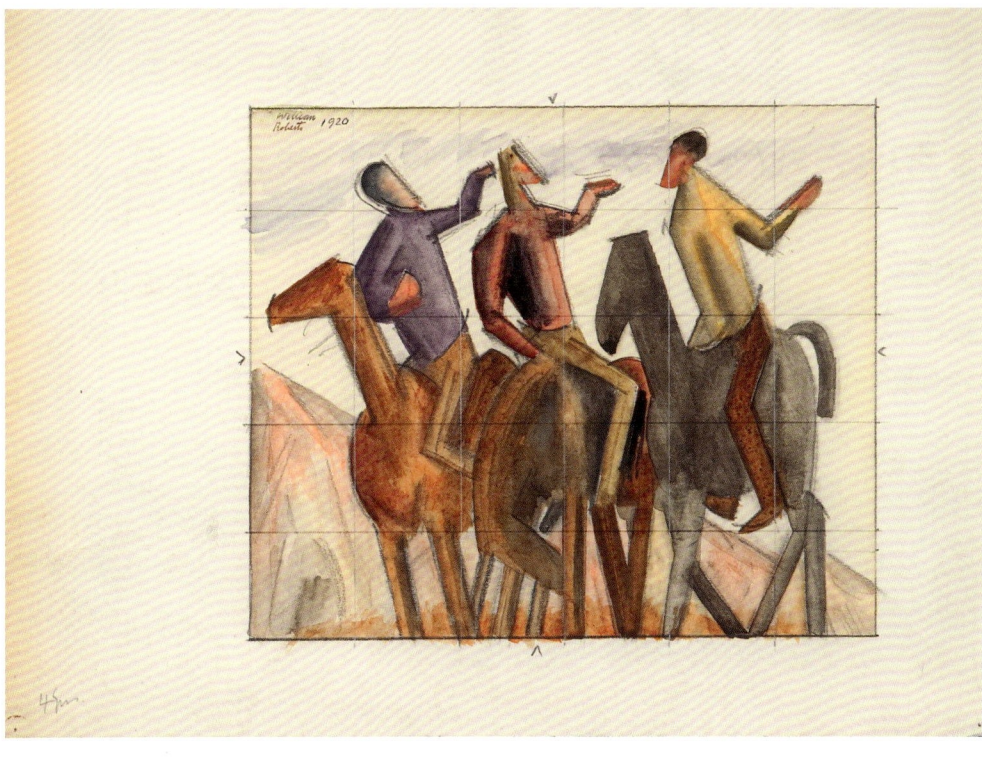

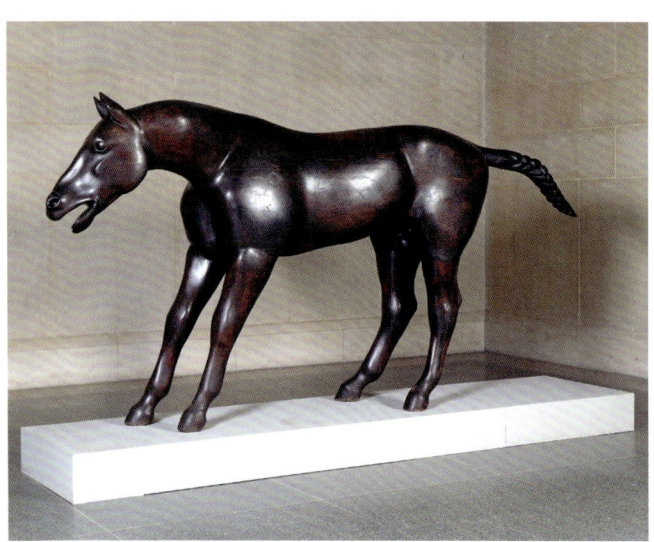

John Skeaping 1901–80
Horse exhibited 1934
Mahogany and pyinkado 181.6 × 388.6 × 67.3

Horse measures just under two metres high and almost four
metres long. It is not attached to a pedestal: only the four feet
hold the immense weight of the sculpture. Skeaping's horse
appears alert and energetic. Newspaper accounts at the time of
its unveiling reported that the animal was based on an English
Thoroughbred, while another added that Skeaping captured the
moment before a race, as a horse prepares to launch forward.
To make the mahogany body, Skeaping cut the trunk of the
reddish-brown timber in half lengthwise and hollowed it out
with an adze. The seam passes along the spine and halfway along
the neck. Skeaping's sculpture brings the imagined horse into
the physical world.

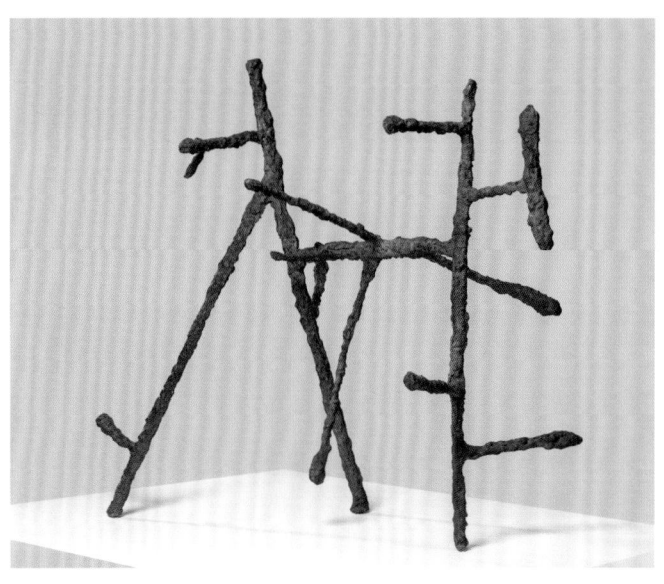

William Turnbull 1922–2012
Horse 1950
Bronze 78 × 91 × 58

While still a student at the Slade School of Fine Art in 1946,
Willian Turnbull made the first of his many depictions of a horse.
Four years later he made *Horse*. Starting with a wire armature,
he built up the mass of the horse in simple and static forms.
The sculpture invites looking from all sides to ascertain which
end is the head and which the tail. It rests daintily on a plinth
on only three legs which, like its body, are delicate and simplified:
a muscled, impressive being is now fragile and indefinable. The
reduction of its physicality disassociates it from symbolism
attached to power and imposing presence. New meanings can
now be ascribed to its form.

Susan Crawford born 1941
Horse and Rider 1973
Lithograph on paper 57.8 × 78.1

A horse and rider are suspended in a moment of wild emotion.
The cause of their behaviour is unknown; with no background
or context given, we are left to focus on their relationship. The
horse's swishing tail and the wash of colour in the circular form
behind the pair evoke the movement of a tornado. The rider
appears to be skilled and accustomed to horses, and sits easily
without the comfort of the saddle or support of stirrups. His
connection with the horse seems fraught, however – with core
muscles drawn in, arms tensed and thighs contracted against the
animal's body, he seems angry and tense. The horse does not match
the rider's rage; instead, its bulging eyes and flattened ears
suggest it is frightened, perhaps startled by its rider's shouting.

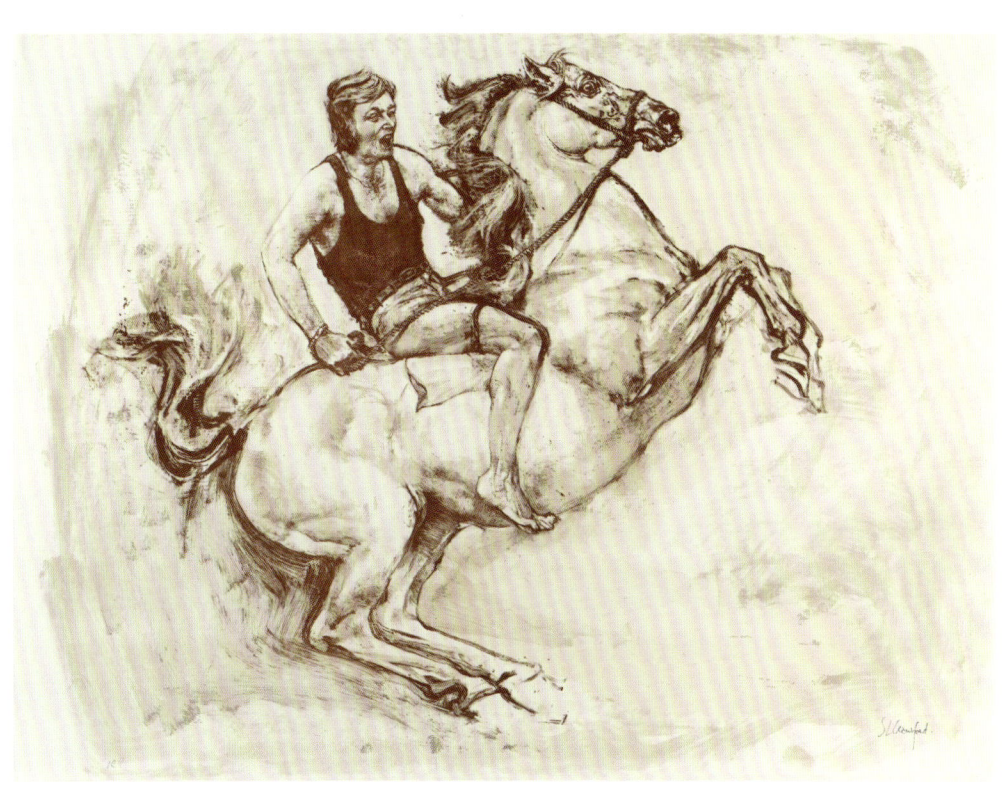

John Piper 1903–92
Photograph of an unidentified child playing on a toy horse
at Sezincote Estate, Gloucestershire c.1930–80
Black and white negative photograph 5.8 × 5.8

A young child in a smart coat rides a push-along toy horse on
a grand private estate. They seem elated on their plush-bodied
pony. The horse can only move forward with the push of a grown
companion – but to the child, it is their version of a real horse,
joining them on an imagined adventure. Perhaps this horse is
pulling a barge along a canal or patrolling city streets, jumping
over obstacles in a steeplechase or galloping towards the ball in
a polo match. The toy horse unlocks their imagination: the way
in which horses and humans have interacted over millennia finds
a new iteration in this child's play.

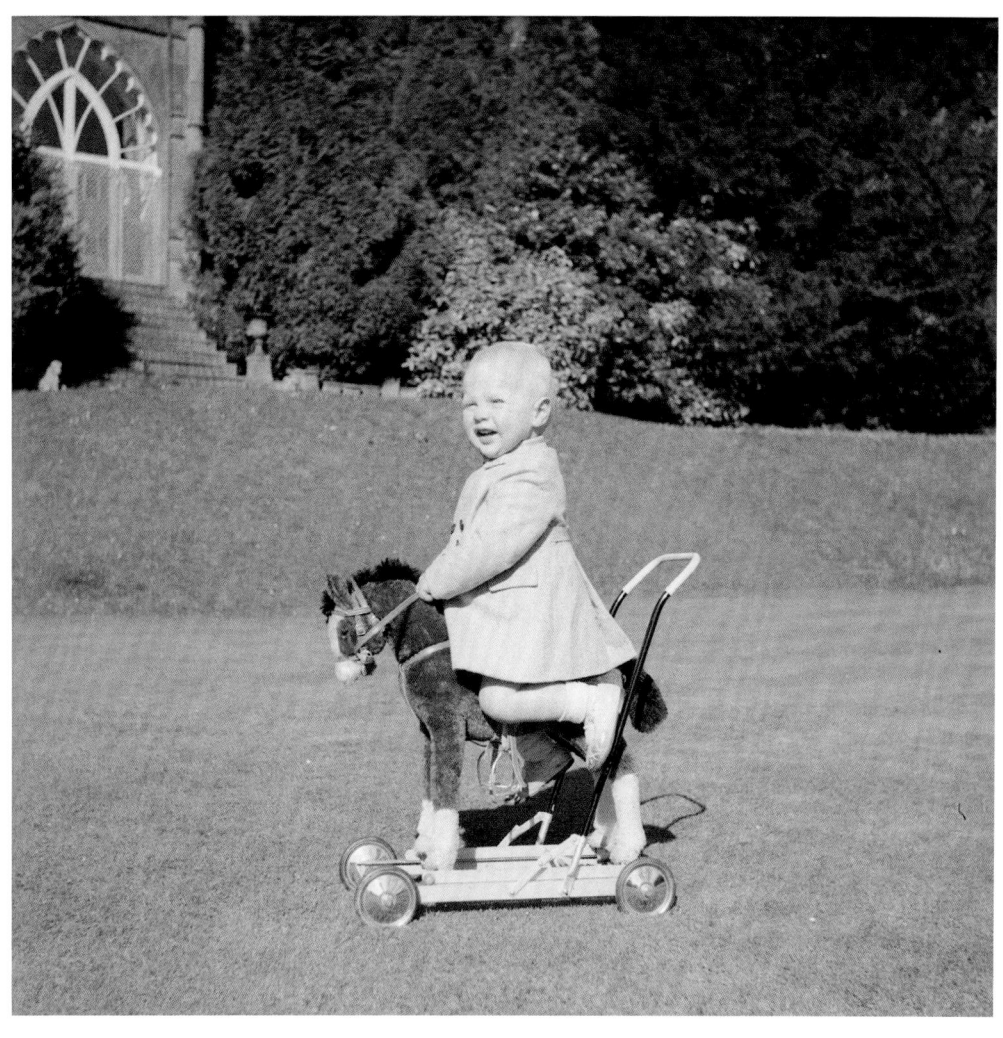

To Tanatswa, Ryan, Samantha,
Panashe, Anesu, Aden, Coen,
Tinomuda-Rose, Malachi and Savannah.

ABOUT THE AUTHOR
Chiedza Mhondoro is Assistant
Curator, British Art at Tate
Britain, specialising in the art of
the eighteenth century and its
social, cultural, political,
economic and international
contexts.

ACKNOWLEDGEMENTS
With thanks to Alice Insley,
Amy Concannon, Tim Batchelor,
Emilia Will, Neil Stewart, Jennifer
Jordan, Sinentokozo Matsebula
and Ronke Oladele.

INDEX OF ARTISTS

First published 2024 by order of the Tate Trustees
by Tate Publishing, a division of Tate Enterprises Ltd,
Millbank, London SW1P 4RG
www.tate.org.uk/publishing

A catalogue record for this book is available from the
British Library

ISBN 978 1 84976 931 0

Distributed in the United States and Canada by ABRAMS,
New York

Library of Congress Control Number applied for

Senior Editor: Emilia Will
Production: Juliette Dupire
Picture Researcher: Roz Hill
Designed by Sandra Zellmer
Colour reproduction by DL Imaging, London
Printed and bound in Italy by Printer Trento S.r.l.

Front cover: Mark Wallinger *Half-Brother (Exit to
Nowhere – Machiavellian)* 1994–5 (detail, see p.113)
Frontispiece: Eric Ravilious *The Vale of the White Horse*
c.1939 (detail, see p.65)
Page 4: Samuel Waller *Sweethearts and Wives* 1882
(detail, see p.51)

Measurements of artworks are given in centimetres,
height before width and depth